The Seagull Sartre Library

The Seagull Sartre Library

The Seagull Sartre Library

VOLUME 4
POLITICAL FICTIONS

JEAN-PAUL SARTRE

TRANSLATED BY
CHRIS TURNER

x

LONDON NEW YORK CALCUTTA

This work is published with the support of
Institut français en Inde – Embassy of France in India

Seagull Books, 2021

Originally published in Jean-Paul Sartre,
Situations I © Éditions Gallimard, Paris, 1947, and
Situations IV © Éditions Gallimard, Paris, 1964

These essays were first published in English translation by Seagull
Books in *Portraits* (2009) and *Critical Essays* (2010)
English translation © Christ Turner, 2009, 2010

ISBN 978 0 8574 2 907 0

British Library Cataloguing-in-Publication Data
A catalogue record for this book is available
from the British Library

Typeset by Seagull Books, Calcutta, India
Printed and bound in the USA by Integrated Books International

CONTENTS

✳

OF RATS AND MEN

> They rectified his squint with glasses, his lisp
> with a metal loop, his stammer with mechanical
> exercises, and he spoke perfectly, but in a voice
> so fast and low that his mother was forever com-
> plaining, 'What are you saying? Talk louder!
> What are you mumbling about now?' and they
> nicknamed him 'Mumbler' . . .[1]

You are about to hear this muted, steady, courteous
voice, and from this moment on you will be able to dis-
tinguish it from all others. To whom does it belong? To
no one. It is as though language had begun speaking all
by itself. There is an occasional mention of the word 'I'
and we think we catch a glimpse of the Speaker of this
Speech, the subject choosing the terms. This is a pure
mirage; the subject of the verb is itself merely an abstract

---

1 Andre Gorz, *The Traitor* (Richard Howard trans.) (London: Verso,
1989) (translation modified). [All subsequent quotations are from
this edition—Trans.]

word; the sentence has gone along its familiar path and has taken a personal slant out of sheer convenience. In fact, *someone is here*: 'a thin fellow with hollow cheeks and eyes, a sloping forehead and chin, a long tortoise's neck arched forward from a slightly stooping back: he moves like a bird with miserly gestures, as if trying to contain his being within himself.' But he says nothing. He is an 'object'. Every proposition rearranges him, designates him. Were it not for this mute creature, his voice would be quite deserted; he lives in it, extends his verbal body through the words; the voice informs us that *he* is anxious, that *he* has completed a philosophical work and that *he* is preparing to take it to a certain Morel's.

You will ask what concern of ours this anonymous whispering can be. We want books that are properly put together, with real authors: in the case of literature, as in that of a trapeze act, our sole pleasure lies in being able to appreciate the artist's work; we attach no more importance to the *frissons* that run through abandoned language than to the wind shaking the reeds. If this is your view, then put down this book. On its last page, indeed, a certain Gorz, emerging from the depths, asserts his retrospective rights over the language that has engendered him. 'I didn't want to make a work of art,' he says. You will readily believe him. Almost as soon as you heard this abandoned voice, you discerned in it both the uncertain flabbiness of natural things and some sort of arid, unselfconscious questing always on the verge of getting bogged down in words. Now, art is a calm image of movement;

when you begin reading a novel or even a confession, everything has long since been settled; 'before' and 'after' are merely conventional markers; the birth and death of love exist simultaneously, each extending into the other in the eternal indistinctness of the moment. To read is to carry out a time transfusion: it is our lives that lend life to the hero; his ignorance of the future and of the perils besetting him is, in reality, our ignorance; it is out of our patience as readers that he manufactures a parasitic span of time for himself, the thread of which we break off and pick up again as the fancy takes us. As for style, that great flourish of the vainglorious, it is death. Its illusory speed carries us back to the author's past. And the author may groan all he likes, he may torture himself before our very eyes, but he feels nothing, he is simply telling his story. By the time he picks up his pen, matters have long since been settled: his friend has betrayed him, his mistress has left him and he has taken the decision to hate them or to hate the human race. He is writing to convey his hatred: style is a hammer that crushes our resistance, a sword to cut our reasoning to shreds. Everything about it is ellipsis, syncope, flea-jumps and false connivance; rhetoric becomes terror; rage and insolence, calculated humiliation and pride control the 'attack' and the crafting of the sentences. The great writer, that madman, hurls himself upon language, subdues it, enslaves it, mistreats it, *for want of a better way*; alone in his study, he is an autocrat. If he streaks a bolt of lightning across his pages that will dazzle twenty generations, it is because he, through this verbal *diktat*, is after the symbol of the respectability and the humble powers that his contemporaries stubbornly refuse to grant him. It is the vengeance of a dead man, for scorn killed him long ago. Behind these lightning strokes lies a dead child who prefers himself to anything else: the child Racine, the child Pascal, the child Saint-Simon—these are our classics. We like to stroll among the tombs of literature, that peaceful cemetery, deciphering the epitaphs and resuscitating eternal meanings momentarily. It is reassuring that such phrases *did* once live: their meaning is fixed forever; they will not take advantage of the brief survival we deign to lend them to move off unexpectedly and drag us towards some unknown future. As for the novelists who are not yet so fortunate as to be in their coffins, they play dead. They will go and find words in their stock ponds, kill them, gut and season them and serve them up to us grilled, *meunière* or *au bleu*.

The Traitor can be regarded as both less and more than a literary undertaking. This Gorz is not dead; he even has the impertinence, at the beginning of his book, not to be born yet. So there is no rhetoric. Who would there be to persuade us? And of what? Nor is there any question of siphoning off our time to sustain a fictional hero or of guiding our dreams with words. There is only this voice: a voice that searches, but does not know what it is searching for; that wants, but does not know what it wants; that speaks in the void, in the dark—perhaps to give a meaning *through words* to the words it has just let slip, or perhaps to conceal its fear.

It is afraid: of that we can be in no doubt. It said, '*He* is afraid, *he* is anxious, because *he* has finished his book.' It aspired to impassiveness, but it was merely a soundscape in which various objective meanings gathered. It enumerated the passions of a hollow-eyed, thin chap, but it did not feel them. We are not fooled: confined initially in this alien body, in *the individual being spoken about*, the passions have spread beyond their envelope; we can no longer pin them down. The whole voice is permeated with anxiety; anxiety accounts for the inert urgency of this mumbling. These groping, scrupulous, modest words are fevered ones: it is the voice of Care that we hear. This time we have understood: the individual *being talked about* is the one *who is speaking*; but the two do not succeed in becoming one. There is at least one man on earth who eats, drinks, works, sleeps—in short, someone who seems just like us, but who is condemned by some obscure, evil spell to remain *another* in his own eyes.

Has his inner life been pounded and ground down to the point where only a swarm of words is left in a decomposed body? Or is his—intact—consciousness so deeply buried that it views him from afar as something alien and does not recognize him? No one knows yet, since this fissured creature is no one. There is the dummy with hollow eyes, this pure object that does not know itself; there is this little tumult of words that unravels in the empty darkness and does not hear itself. Who, in fact, is this voice speaking to? To us? Certainly not. To address human beings, you have first of all to be fully a human being. It is not concerned with being listened to: it is the fissure itself gaping ever wider as it strives to close; it is a dropped stitch in language that has begun to unravel. Without reference points and prompted by a nameless anxiety, the words perform their labour: if they strive determinedly to designate this carcase of a man, it is because they are obscurely trying to lay hold of it, to dissolve it into them. The voice was born of a danger: one must either lose oneself or win the right to speak in the first person.

That is why this soliloquy is so disconcerting: we stumble upon it unawares. You will smile at my naivety. You will say, 'After all, Gorz *did publish* his book.' Yes, *when there was* a Gorz to make the decision; but he has added nothing and taken nothing away from this beginning, which seemed to be going nowhere and was intended for no one. Whenever I chattered too much as a child, I remember being told, 'Be quiet, you babbling stream.' And there'll be a babbling stream flowing through you, made up of these long caterpillar-crawling sentences, interrupted by asides, swelled by the addition of further retrospective considerations, abbreviated by erasures for reasons of scruple or regret and suddenly upended by leaps into the past. Where is Order? Where is Ceremony? Where is mere politeness? Vainly would you try to cling on to the earlier declarations: they are constantly being transformed by the ones that follow: on page 80 you learn that what you read on page 30 is not what *one* really thought—*one* merely supposed one did. And on page 150 you learn *one* did not even believe it, and on page 170 that *one* hadn't in fact written it but that *one* wrote a certain sentence imagining *one* was writing another; and on page 200 you learn that the imagined and written meanings are strictly interchangeable and are, in fact, both wrong. But you should not assume we are witnessing a confession that is initially mendacious and gradually discovers its own sincerity. There is neither confessor nor confessional—nor even anything to confess. When the voice struck up—I know this and can attest to it—it had nothing to say and its truth did not exist. It uttered words at random, since a beginning had to be made: these words are transparent, they refer only to themselves. And do not try to find some ruse of exposition in this artless stammering: no undertaking could be more sincere or less artificial. It begins in anguish, in penury, *here* before your very eyes and with these very words; it wanders off and we wander off with it; *it is true* that it loses itself and will re-find itself; *it is true* that it breaks free from itself and grows richer.

Being used to the exercises of the mind, we believe, from the very first words, that we grasp the movement of this thought, the intention governing the construction of a paragraph: these rapid anticipations, these implicit conjectures, these expectations are what ordinarily enable us to understand the way of the world and men's actions. So we leapfrog the developments that are to come and settle ourselves comfortably at the finishing line, waiting for this language to unfold itself. But in the present instance this is no way at all to proceed. We had discovered an intention and we were not wrong to do so. But that intention changed along the way: there was no one there to maintain it; 'the Master is in the Styx' or, rather, 'in Limbo'; there are these snippets of sonorous inanity which change as they find body, each of which, by its mere presence, modifies all the others. Leaning against the last milepost, we see the verbal flow moving towards us, then suddenly it gathers, contracts and slides off down another slope, leaving us in the lurch. The indefinite recurrence of such disappointments will cause us at first to see a prattling disorder in what will later seem to be an order in the making.

For it *is* an order, this slow, unpredictable wandering: it is a truth in the process of becoming, organizing itself in minute detail; it is a whole human existence passing from the abstract to the concrete, from poverty to riches, from the universal to the individual, from anonymous objectivity to subjectivity. There are excuses for our astonishment: books are dead bodies and yet here is one which, hardly have we picked it up, becomes a living creature. We have, of course, had to open it, turn the pages and revive the signs; but the mere movement of reading will give rise to an unforeseeable event, with neither its moments nor its end given in advance; you imagine you are lending it your own time, and it is the book that imposes its time on you; you will discover the laws of this venturesome discourse only as it generates them, but you will know at the same time that they will not stop changing and that the whole system will transform those laws even as it dances to their tune.

This flinty, muffled—breaking—voice will live on in your ears: its slowness is a genuine speed, since it is guiding us towards a *real future*, the *only* one that is not a masquerade of memories; towards a place no one knows, which does not exist, and yet *will be*. It strips down its 'appearances': neither lukewarm, nor flabby, nor fluid, it discloses to us the inflexible order of *enrichment*. Each sentence gathers all the preceding ones into it; each is the living milieu in which all the others breathe, endure and change. Or there is, rather, only one sentence, moving over all kinds of terrain, nourished by all soils, ever thicker, rounder and denser, which will swell until it bursts, until it becomes a human being. At every moment, it runs a *real* risk: it may be that it explodes, that it comes to a woeful halt and collapses back on itself, a great inert ball, frozen in the desert of the present. We feel this risk within ourselves; we read anxiously. The book seems, of course, to have been completed; after this page there are others. But what does that prove? Everything may peter out into nothing or, worse still, get hopelessly bogged down. What reassures us, however, is that, beyond the hesitations of life and language, we glimpse a sharp, ice-cold, arid passion, a steel wire stretched between the lacerations of the past and the uncertainty of the future. An inhuman, blind passion—a questing malaise, a manic silence at the heart of language—drives a hole in the reader's time and pulls this whole cavalcade of words along behind it; we shall trust it.

Since the work of art shouts to the four winds the name of the artist, that great dead man who determined it all, *The Traitor* is not a work of art. It is an event, a sudden precipitation, a disorder of words ordering themselves. You hold in your hands this surprising object—*a work* in the process of creating *its* author. Of that author we know nothing, save this one negative feature: he will not be—cannot be—that sacred monster called the Writer. If, at the end of his struggle, he finds himself, it will be as everyman, as a man like the rest, for the voice is in search of a man, not a monster. Do not, then, expect that *gesture* that is style; everything here is in action. But if, in our great authors, you enjoy a certain savour for words, a particular cast of phrasing, a depiction of feelings and thought, then read *The Traitor.* You will, at first, lose everything, but all will be restored to you. Its abandonment, its passionate questing, its breaking— all these things lend an inimitable tone to this voice. In this subjectless writing, the radical impossibility of style ultimately becomes a transcendence of all known styles, or, if you prefer, the style of death gives way to a style of life.[2]

Some will not like what Gorz has done. We like those who like us: if you want to be read, you have to give yourself, to nip the words surreptitiously so as to send a tremor through them, contrive a husky-voiced affection: but *he*, the object, the third person, the third-rater, how could he like us? How could the voice like us? We are dealing with a man split in two, who is trying to reconcile the parts of himself with each other: it's an occupation that leaves no time for leisure; the whoring is for tomorrow, if that's possible. To which you will doubtless reply that you haven't much time yourself and soldering problems don't interest you. But what do you know?

I sometimes read science-fiction stories. And I always enjoy them: they give a precise indication of just how frightened we are of ourselves. One story in particular captivated me—about a human landing on Venus. The colonizers-to-be have barely stepped out of their rocket when they set about joyously hunting the natives, their future colonial subjects, though these do not initially show themselves. You can imagine the pride of the King of Nature, his exhilaration at his triumph and his

---

2 I do not claim to establish Gorz's superiority, but his originality. Along with everyone else, I love death as much as life, for both are part of our fate.

new freedom. But everything quickly collapses in the face of an unbearable realization: the conquerors are behind bars and every move they make is anticipated. The paths they take are ones preordained for them. The Venusians, watching unseen over the glass cage, are subjecting these higher mammals to intelligence tests. This, it seems to me, is our shared condition, except that we are our own Venusians and our own guinea-pigs. Open *The Traitor*: you are would-be colonizers; you look on, with a shake of your head, at a strange animal—perhaps a native—running around in a great panic on the surface of Venus. But I dare say it wouldn't be two minutes before you see that the native is a rat and that rat is none other than yourself. The book was a trap and we have fallen into it; at present, we are hightailing it through the corridors of an oversized maze under the gaze of the experimenters—that is to say, under *our own* gaze. The experiment is under way: the question at issue is whether there is in this falsified world a single act of which we can say, '*I* did that.' Can we *recognize* our undertakings? Is their nature not *changed* by being brought to fruition? Is it not *others* who pursue them in our stead, others dearer to us than ourselves, who are nourished by our blood? Scarcely has this stranger in my heart of hearts decided my behaviour for me than I hear the shouts of the crowd within: a great ferment seizes hold of all these people I do not know; they condemn my initiative and protest that I must take sole responsibility for it. 'I am another,' says the voice of the Traitor. I find it extremely restrained; in its place, I would say that I am *others* and would speak of myself in the third-person plural. Each of my acts, registering itself in the passivity of being, forms itself into a whirligig whose imperious inertia defines me as *its man*, or, in other words, *its slave*—the other that I have to be to give it its initial impulsion and keep on renewing it *ad infinitum*. My most casual acts, my most sincere commitments, produce only inanimate patterns; I have to slip into these merry-go-rounds and move around inside them, like a showground horse, to make them turn. *He*, the author writing this preface, is an Other at this very moment, an Other I do not like. I enjoyed the book and I agreed to preface it, because one always has to pay to have the right to like what one does. But as soon as I took up my pen, an invisible little carrousel was set in motion just above the paper: it was the foreword as literary genre that calls for the attentions of the specialist, a fine old fellow, all passion spent, a member of the Académie française. Was I *not* a member of the Académie? No matter: *he* would become one for the nonce. How could one dare to present another person's book, unless one were at death's door? *He* got inside the character; he turned himself into the great diaphanous-and-admiring elder; *he* wrote all of the foregoing with a long, pale hand manipulating my stubby little one. He sinks his tentacles into me, he sucks up my words and ideas to extract from them his somewhat dated blessings. If I try to wrest myself from his grasp and write naturally, it is worse: I no longer have any naturalness—*he* sifts it and transforms it into *bonhomie*. He will continue to hold the pen until the end of this exercise and then vanish. But, whatever I may undertake subsequently, be it pamphlet, lampoon or autobiography, other Vampires await me, future intermediaries between my consciousness and the written page.

At least I can hope the intruder will go away. But sometimes he stays; sometimes I fall victim to his long-term installation—even collude in it. One day, *Mirandola* found himself compelled to publish, under the pseudonym *Jouvence*, one of those angry, healthy books that exhort their reader to show courage and which, for that reason, is called 'courageous'. The work met with some success. Reading between the lines, sad, weary men saw an austere, sacred figure who restored their hope. In short, Mirandola's book, as it cooled, created Jouvence, its real author. Jouvence is recognized today as a general influence for good, his virtues are taught in our primary schools; he is seen as a national treasure and often represents France abroad. He lives off Mirandola and, through him, Mirandola has died. The other day, at some first night or other, there was only a measly little foldaway seat reserved for the two of them. Now, Mirandola is modest by nature—almost shy. Yet he took the offence to heart and, shaking with rage, made a scene. 'Personally, I wouldn't have said anything,' he explained as he was leaving, 'but I *couldn't* let them do *that* to Jouvence.'

What wrong had he done? What wrong have you done? After all, we don't wish these undesirable guests upon ourselves: it is the Others who force them on us. The others or the instruments of the Others, those stiff fingers constantly pointing at us: it is his leather bag and the patient that make a hare-brained, fat man into the *Doctor*, that angelic dictator, that enlightened despot, who seeks to do us good despite ourselves and after whose orders, admonishments and adorable severity we hanker.

We sometimes feel the urge to muzzle the Vampires and show ourselves as we are: no one is listening; it is *They* who are expected. In response to this disappointment, or to the general indifference, we say wryly to ourselves, 'Well, if that's what everyone wants,' and then we release the monsters. It always ends badly. In the early days after the war, I met a foreign painter. He had come over from London and we were chatting in a cafe. He was another Traitor—at least, he thought he was. He liked himself so little that people detested him: it was his name they liked. I found him very charming. Weak and authoritarian, distrustful and naïve, madly proud and filled with shame, wicked and affectionate, fascinated by his fame and inconvenienced by it, he was still quite astounded to have a considerable body of work behind him which, nonetheless, he scorned. This Don Quixote could not gain his own esteem unless, on another terrain, he won a battle that he knew he would never even manage to engage. Everything ended, in fact, two years later in gales of laughter. Unstable, unhappy and romantic, he was dependent on the hour, on the light, on a note of music, on women and, above all, on men—all men. *All working together*, we could have saved him; lacking that unanimity, he wavered between haughtiness and a defenceless kindness: sometimes, to forget that old, poorly medicated venereal disease, his Treason, he allowed himself to be swallowed whole by the prestigious being he represented for other people; on those occasions, all that remained of him was a gleaming insect. At other times, fear, affection and good faith changed him into himself, into an unexceptional man who painted. That day, sitting at another table, was a little old man who could not take his eyes off him. I knew him to be one of the painter's compatriots, also an *émigré*, but one who had not enjoyed the same good fortune. In the end, no longer able to restrain himself, the old man rose, came over and introduced himself to my companion, who, with his guard down, innocently returned his smile. The fame and the genius were together extinguished; there were just two exiles there, acknowledging, but not knowing, each other, neither of them happy, talking as friends.

It was the more unfortunate of the two who re-lit the halo around his interlocutor's head: there had been a misunderstanding; it hadn't been the man he had been addressing but the Painter. We must not ask too much of artists: summoned up by too manifest a respect, by some servile inflections, the Great Man appeared. He was sheer perfection: understanding, modest, so simple in his genius that he put his companion to flight: the latter hurriedly picked up the papers lying on the table and left the cafe with a rancorous, disappointed air, not understanding that he had engineered his own downfall. We remained alone and, after an embarrassed silence, the great personage murmured these words which I shall never forget: 'Another failure!' This meant, 'He had told himself he would forget his name, his fame and his voluminous presence, that *he* would simply be an exile with another companion in exile.' But since he was expected to play the Incomparable Artist, *he* resigned himself and lent his body and voice to that Other who is not even his own, *personal* parasite but one that simultaneously sucks the blood of a good thousand people from Peking to Moscow and from Paris to Valparaiso. And he heard that Other speaking in his own mouth with the terrible sweetness that meant: 'But no, it's nothing, I'm nothing, I'm no better than you, it's just that lady luck has smiled on me.' And he realized he had once again missed the *opportunity*; it might recur each day at any moment, and every day, on each occasion, he would miss it.

The test is not over—we have not finished trotting round the maze, the voice has not finished speaking. The investigation does not concern these tourists, these travellers who inhabit us by the month or by the day. We shall not be asked to account for the furnished rooms, the mirror-lined salons we let out to our passing clientele. Everyone will be released after the customary identity-checks except for one mysterious guest who claims to be the jailer but who is, in reality, merely our oldest tenant. This is the character the voice insists on calling 'He'. And listen to that voice—already it is no longer quite the same. In the beginning, it confined itself to commenting on the occupant's actions; then it revealed that that particular character was under observation; it described the tests he had been subjected to and published the results. Stronger now, tenacious, at times even violent, it is an *interrogating* voice: the Venusians have turned into cops and the rats into suspects. Naturally, we are told at first that we are merely *witnesses* in a police enquiry. No one seems concerned with us. It's a certain Gorz who's in the hot seat. His name has just been mentioned. There's no let-up to his questioning; they try to break his alibis, to force him to contradict himself. What was he doing in Vienna on a particular day in winter 1936? And before that, as a small child? And afterwards, at the time of the *Anschluss*? He acknowledges he went about with young Nazis; that he admired them. Why? He claims he subsequently broke with them. Is that really true? Did he do so of his own accord? Can he say, 'I *broke* with them'? Wasn't he forced into it by circumstances? By his *objective nature*? And where does that nature come from? From whom? From what? Silent and embarrassed, we watch the questioning and do our best to feel indiscreet. What good fortune if we could say, '*I* wasn't in Vienna in Chancellor Dollfuss' day; that business has nothing to do with me.' But no: we are stuck and we know it. At the point when we demonstrate to the officers that our presence in the torture chamber can be explained as a simple misunderstanding, we have long since begun to confess. Torturers and victims—as ever it is we, the cops, who 'put' the traitor 'to the question'. But as soon as he starts to talk, as soon as he denounces his first 'inhabitant'—that misshapen dwarf who may, we think, have died, or who may in fact be hiding (and it may be his puckish face that has just pressed itself against the window and is making rude gestures at us)— we suddenly remember the little cripple that has lived inside us for so long and try to reconstruct the suspicious circumstances of his disappearance. In 1920, I existed and *he* still existed: *who, then*, had so cruelly mutilated him? I remember I didn't like him much. Then I stopped seeing him; there was a murder, I think. But which of us killed the other? The voice is still speaking: it has found words for the fissure running through us; the first guilty parties left their fingerprints on a knife and it will not be long before we identify them.

It seems, in fact, that there are still savages on Earth who are so stupid as to see their newborn children as reincarnated ancestors. The weapons and necklaces of the dead are waved over the infant's head; if, in response, he moves, a great shout goes up: great uncle is reborn! The old man will suckle, will soil the straw beneath him and they will call him by his name. The survivors from his generation will take pleasure in seeing their comrade of the hunt and the battlefield waving his little legs about and exercising his lungs. As soon as he can speak, they will inculcate memories of the dead man into him. Strict training will restore his previous character; he will be reminded that *he* was angry, cruel or big-hearted and will remain convinced of it, despite experience suggesting otherwise. What barbarity: they take a living child and sew him up in a dead man's skin; he will stifle in this senile childhood, where he has no other occupation than the exact reproduction of avuncular gestures, no other hope than to poison future childhoods after his death. After this, should we be surprised that he speaks of himself with the greatest of precaution, under his breath and often in the third person? This sad character is fully aware that he is his own great-uncle.

These backward aborigines are to be found in Fiji, Tahiti and New Guinea, in Vienna, Paris and Rome— indeed, wherever there are human beings. They are called parents. Long before we were born, even before they conceived us, our families defined our personas. They applied the word 'he' to us years before we could say 'I'. We existed first *as absolute objects*. Through our families, society assigned us a situation, a being, a set of rules; social struggles and the contradictions of history determine in advance the character and destiny of the coming generations.

Algeria, 1935: the parents are exploited, oppressed and reduced to poverty in the name of a racism that

refuses them the status of human being; Arabic is taught
as a dead language; French schools are so few in number
that the great majority of Algerians are illiterate. Rejected
by France, without rights, culture or past, they find suc-
cour only in religion, in the negative pride of a nascent
nationalism. Are their sons, the *fellagha* of 1957, not
made in advance? And who made them but the colonial-
ists? Who, from Bugeaud's[3] time onwards, prescribed
this destiny of anger, despair and blood for them? Who
built these infernal machines that must one day explode
and blow up colonialism? The roles are there—everywhere—just waiting for the human beings to fill them:
for the one, the role of Jew, for another, the part of
landowner. But these functions are still too abstract:
within the family, they are particularized. We have all
been forced to reincarnate *at least one* dead person, gen-
erally a child that has fallen victim to its nearest and
dearest, killed at a young age, his desolate ghost outliving
himself in adult form: our own father or mother, those
living dead. Barely is he out of the womb and every child
is mistaken *for someone else*; he is pulled and pushed
around to force him into his persona, like those children
the *Comprachicos* jammed into porcelain vases to prevent
them from growing. At least, you will say, *they* were not
their molesters' sons: sometimes they were bought, often
they were stolen. That was doubtless the case: but who
is not, more or less, a stolen child? Stolen from the

---

3 Thomas Robert Bugeaud (1784–1849): appointed Governor-
General of Algeria in 1840. [Trans.]

world, stolen from his fellow man, stolen from himself? The custom has perpetuated itself: out of stolen children, child thieves are made.

All this we knew: we had always known it; a lone voice kept telling us it was so, but we preferred to say nothing. It spoke in the desert—in *our* desert: *he* did this or that in our stead and we were *his* straw men. Out of cowardice or connivance, we said, 'I did it.' And everyone pretended to believe us, on the understanding that we would return the favour. In this way, for millennia, humanity, ashamed of giving in to fear and blackmail, has hidden from itself the revolving racket that has lived off its back. Fortunately, someone has just spilled the beans: a traitor, a man like one of those American dockers who, from disgust at their own cowardice, inform on the gang exploiting them and are found, shortly afterwards, in the Hudson, washed up on the tide. A traitor: a fissured character like all of us, but one who could no longer bear the duplicity. He has broken the silence and refused to underwrite the acts of the intruder assuming his identity—refused to say 'I'. This has immediately left the *Others* naked—the *zar*s, the *loa*s, the black angels, the sons of Cain, all our parasites. Naked but not dead: we are torn between scandal and terror; at any minute, we expect the Union to strike back and bump off the 'stoolpigeon'. We have, in fact, gained no victory: we have merely found the cracks in ourselves once more, rediscovered our occupying forces. But we have lost our illusions: we thought that the little gnawing noise came in through our ears. But no: it was born in our hearts. This time we recognize the universal murmuring of slavish minds, the Human Voice—and we are not about to forget it.

This does not, of course, prevent the Traitor from belonging to a very peculiar species: he has his own way of being just anyone. Neither the Foolish Scholars nor the Preening Heroes have chosen to take up residence inside him. If he speaks of himself in the third person, he does so not from excess but from lack: he would regard the measured acts performed in his name as *his own* if only he could find the motives for them. He has carried out a hundred searches, but never with any result. The conclusion has to be that he cares about nothing. *He* travels without wishing to travel; *he* meets people; *he* visits their homes; *he* has them round without enjoying their company; at other times *he* goes to ground, *he* shuts himself away without any wish to be alone. Is he merely sated? He cannot be: to turn one's back on the good things of life, one must first have cared for them. And, above all, let us not criticize him for his 'seen-it-all-before' attitude. For he doesn't give the impression of having been or seen anything. He hasn't left the spot: that is his real misfortune. And why not? Because he hadn't enough desire. His heart shows no trace of that haughty dissatisfaction that has served three generations of French writers as an alibi. The Infinite, the eternal Elsewhere, the Dream—he doesn't, thank God, give a damn for these things. I know people who feel entitled to scorn the world because they compare it with some perfect prototype. But the Traitor scorns nothing and no one. So are we talking of the 'empty suitcase' Drieu la Rochelle[4] spoke of? No: the suitcase trick was fine for the inter-war years: you opened it, you asked the onlookers to see for themselves that there was nothing inside but pyjamas and a toothbrush. We know today that it had a false bottom, that it was used for trafficking arms and drugs: the gilded youth craftily hid in it everything that could serve the destruction of the human race and hasten the coming of the Inhuman. But the Traitor will have nothing to do with blowing up the world: the Inhuman is already *his lot* because he doesn't share the same ends as other human beings. In a word, I class him among the Indifferent. This is a group of recent origin, its representatives are no older than thirty and no one knows yet what will become of them. But we must say right away that we shall fail to understand them if we insist on ascribing to them an aristocratic nonchalance. What sets them apart is their bustling zeal. Gorz holds down a job, cultivates his body and mind; he has taken a wife. If you met him at the Palais de Justice or the Stock Exchange, carrying his smart briefcase, you would take him for a man of your own kind. He is punctual, even finicky, in his work, and no one is more affable. He shows just a hint of reserve in his daily dealings, which his colleagues

---

4 Pierre Drieu la Rochelle (1893–1945): prominent French fascist novelist and essayist; wrote *La Valise vide* (The Empty Suitcase) in 1921. [Trans.]

smilingly explain away as shyness; but if you ask him a favour, he will drop everything and run—race—to perform it. The most superficial people will regard him as insignificant: he does not, in fact, speak much; *he is like everyone*; this self-effacement and this perfectly imitated similarity to others will ensure his popularity. But when we examine him closer, the impostor is unmasked by his zealousness. Most people, sharing a conviction that they are human beings (one that has been handed down, since Adam, from father to son), treat their human nature rather negligently; they have such an ancient, uncontested entitlement to it that they calmly follow their personal inclinations with a certainty that they can take a pee if they want to or kill quite humanely. But the Indifferent individual knows no inclinations; whether he is having a drink or fighting, he has to make his mind up to do so; he drinks without thirst, takes revenge without anger for an affront he has not felt—*in order to do as the others do*. His first impulse is to have no impulse: this is what has to be ceaselessly hidden and denied. Terrified of falling to the level of the angels or of tamed animals, this curious product of our societies strives to imitate the Adamites in every respect. In so doing, he loses himself. In an excellent little book in which he told the story of his war, Paulhan called himself an 'assiduous warrior'.[5] The Indifferent one becomes suspect for the simple reason that he is an 'assiduous' human being.

---

5 Jean Paulhan, *Le guerrier appliqué* (Paris: Sansot, 1917).

Too assiduous to be honest: if he wants to be taken for my fellow man that is because he *is not*. So, might we say the human community contains fake human beings who are indistinguishable from the real ones? How, in that case, can we know whether the real ones exist? Who will check their *bona fides*? I've heard it said that man is the future of man and, on other occasions, that man is his past: I've never heard it said that man is man's present. We are all fakes. For the second time, the Traitor has let the cat out of the bag: by the passion he puts into *making himself* human, he reminds us that our species does not exist.

The author of this book is, as one might suspect, a rat. And, moreover, a rat possessed. By another rat? By the Rat-in-itself? No, this Other, of which a lone voice speaks to us constantly, this pure object, this receding perspective, this absence—is Man, our tyrant. We are unmasked as rats that are prey to Man. The insane undertaking of the Indifferent one becomes immediately apparent: it is our undertaking. We are all running after a ghost in the corridors of an experimental maze and Gorz is in the lead. If he catches and eats this parasite he has long been feeding with his anxieties and weariness, if he absorbs it into his own substance, our species is possible. Somewhere, between the angels and the rats, it is being born; we *shall* get out of the maze.

Once again, the aim of the book has changed. It is not a question of knowing life now, but of changing it.

We are not yet the ones being addressed, but, like it or not, it is we who are being asked the fundamental question: by what activity can an 'accidental individual'[6] achieve, within himself and for everyone, human personhood? As I have already pointed out, this work has been organized like a machine with 'feedback': the present is constantly transforming the past from whence it came. In the first pages of the book, it seemed the voice was taking up words at random, just anywhere, to escape anxiety and so that there should at least be *something* behind it—anything but silence. And it was true: *at that moment* it was true. But the question of the human being was posed and, with it, a new light is cast over the beginning of the undertaking; a change takes place: *before the voice*, Gorz already existed, he was already pained by his indifference and combated it with the means at his disposal. Suddenly, he changes tactics and reverses his relation to himself. That break represents in itself an absolute event; but we would be wrong to see it as an inner adventure whose chief merit would be to have given rise to the book: it is, in fact, *in* the book that the adventure takes place; it is through it and by it that it develops and becomes conscious of itself. *The Traitor* does not claim to *tell us* the story of a convert; it *is* the conversion itself.

---

6 The expression is Marx's in *German Ideology*. [*Die Deutsche Ideologie*, 1845–46; first published in 1932—Trans.]

Gorz is thirty-two. For thirty-two years, whatever he did, it immediately seemed to him he could have done the opposite and the outcome would have been the same—that is to say, worthless or, worse, meaning- less. For thirty-two years his existence has escaped him; he has no other evidence of it than an insurmountable bore- dom: I am bored, therefore I exist. But he has deliberated on the matter; he has searched and he believes he has found the response. He said to himself,

> Since I'm from nowhere, no group, no project, since I'm the exile from all groups and all pro- jects, there is only the following alter-native: to be on the fringes of society and history, the supernumerary of the human race, reduced to *ennui*, to the acute awareness of the contingency of everything around me; or to raise myself, in my mind, to the absolute—in other words, to ground everything philosophically as a moment of the spiritual adventure and, having done this, having started out from this speculative interest, to regain a taste for the concrete; . . . I can con- nect with . . . the real only by starting out from the Idea.

In other words, because he is made in such a way that he doesn't feel he has any particular desires, he will turn his indifference to advantage: for want of being able to be—or wanting to be (nothing is decided yet)—*a certain* Gorz, he will make himself Universal Man. He will determine his behaviour by concepts and will obey this rule: act always in such a way that the circumstances and the moment serve as a pretext for your acts, in order to bring about, both within and outside you, the generality of the human species. It was for this reason that he undertook to write a work of philosophy at the age of twenty: when you are immunized from birth against the violence of fear, concupiscence or anger, you must either do nothing or ground everything in reason—even the act of opening an umbrella if it is raining.

Everything is explained now and no one will be surprised any longer at his betrayal: he is one of those fellows who have their heads full of words, who analyse everything, who always want to know the whys and the wherefores—a critical, destructive mind. In a word, a filthy intellectual. The point cannot be denied; that is even why I like him: I am one too. A literary paper asked the prince of counterfeiting what he hated the most. He had no hesitation: 'Intellectuals'. I am amiably disposed towards this counterfeiter: he is a true poet and a good man. But I do wonder what got into him that day. Everyone knows his hunted airs, his monologues on destiny, on time, on life, these congestions of words in his throat, purple patches from a perpetual, imploring anthology; his fascinating hands that are words too, their palms turning outward to plead for forgiveness; his thinking, vexed and tired, that presses on regardless, jumping nimbly from one idea to another, not noticing it is merely spinning round inside its cage; these stunning improvisations whose groundlines are to be found in the previous day's writings, which, as they fade, allow us to glimpse the incurable sadness of a frozen stare. This is a man who seeks out a tribunal merely to corrupt it: meeting you, he appoints you judge and jury, spares you no detail of his conduct and will not let you leave until you have acquitted him. But do not be deceived: he knows everything. The sentence he is trying to avoid is the one he knows he passed on himself at the beginning of the century. He knows he is doing hard labour for it and has been for fifty years, for he has condemned himself to plead into old age the cause his adolescence judged lost. What would you call this Devil's Advocate but an *intellectual*?

Of course, I know others who like to set the great silences of the earth, or of the peasants, against such chatter. But if you open them up—what a din! Their heads are buzzing with the words to describe other people's silences. Gorz is the first, I think, to have formulated the problem concretely; and I am grateful to him for it. It matters little that one speaks about language or silence, about the confused intuitions of the poet or clear ideas: what counts is that these speakers are compelled to speak. To defend the dark corners of the heart, the counterfeit man put forward more arguments than Kant to establish the claims of Reason. He was forced to: speeches, concepts, reasoning—these are our lot. Why? Because intelligence is neither a gift nor a defect: it is a drama or, if you prefer, a provisional solution that turns, most often, into a life sentence. Someone once told our traitor, 'You stink of intelligence the way some people stink from their armpits.' And it's true: intelligence stinks. But no more than stupidity: there are odours to suit every taste. Stupidity smells like a wild animal, intelligence like a human being. The fact is that some riven, exiled, condemned individuals attempt to overcome their conflicted natures and loneliness by pursuing the insane image of unanimity. It is this that is reflected in their eyes, shyly offered in their smiles. Unanimity over everything and nothing: the appeal is there, permanently etched on their faces; whatever they say, their voices call for universal agreement. But human beings, laden as they are with particularities, densely packed interests and passions, loathe the idea that someone wants to dissolve their differences and hatreds in the purely formal harmony of assent.

And then, intelligence is meticulous. It wants to start everything over again from the beginning, even the things everyone can do: it takes walking and breathing apart and puts them together again; it learns how to wash, how a nose is blown—all from first principles. It is intelligence that makes intellectuals seem like severely disabled people undergoing rehabilitation. But we have to show some understanding here: each of them is reinventing intelligence to compensate for the enormous clearance sale of all their drives and doggedness. They need it to replace the signals that weren't etched into their flesh, the habits that weren't bestowed on them, the paths that weren't cleared for them—in short, they need it *in order to live*. I remember seeing a puppy after its cerebellum had been partially removed: it could move around the room and seldom bumped into the furniture, but it had become reflective: the animal established its itinerary carefully and thought long and hard before evading an obstacle; it took it a lot of time and thought to accomplish the movements it previously made quite unconsciously. In the language of the day, they said its cortex had taken over the functions of the lower centres: it was, in short, an intellectual dog. I don't know whether it was very useful or very harmful to its fellows but we can quite well imagine that it had lost what another exile, Genet, so aptly termed 'sweet native confusion'; in a word, it had either to die or reinvent the dog. And we de-brained rats are so constituted that we have to either die or reinvent man. We are, as it happens, perfectly well aware that man will constitute himself without us, through labour and struggle, that our models become outdated overnight, and that nothing will remain of them in the finished product, not even a knuckle-bone. On the other hand, that making would be done blindly—by cobbling things together and patching them up—if we de-cerebrated individuals were not there constantly repeating that we must work from principles, that it isn't a question of making-do and mending but hewing and building; that our species will, in a word, be either the concrete universal or nothing at all.

Gorz's intelligence strikes you at the very first glance: it is one of the nimblest, acutest intelligences I know; he must have had great need of this instrument to have honed it to this point. Yet, when he sets about writing his philosophical treatise, he does not avoid contradiction, as is the case with intellectuals. He wants to act as a function of the human condition alone. Yet, as soon as acts are accomplished, they are buried in the particular: what remains is the fortuitous realization of one possibility out of a thousand. But why, precisely, just *this one*? The worst of it is that it compromises him: he cannot even breathe without adding a new touch to the model-less portrait that is none other than his self-portrait. He would have to become all possible Gorzes at once for these empty equivalences to cancel each other out, to be *only man* by becoming *the whole of man*. But no, 'We are born several and we die one only,' says Paul Valéry's Socrates.[7] Gorz cannot prevent himself from living, or from shrinking with use: his universal intelligence outstrips his personal adventure and looks on with distaste as the physiognomy emerges of that Gorz who will be '*one only*'. It rejects it; it does not even want to recognize it; it would joyfully have accepted him being just anyone. Yet he is not even that: a succession of accidents has lent him a definite individuality that is distinguished by little trifles from the others.

---

7 Paul Valéry, *Eupalinos* (Paris: Gallimard, 1944), p. 71. Valéry's Socrates actually makes this assertion in the singular: 'I told you that I was born *several* and I died *one*.'

We—that is to say, we intellectuals—are all familiar with this distracted, cloying anxiety. We thought ourselves universal because we toyed with concepts and then, suddenly, we see our shadows at our feet; we are *here*, we are doing *this* and not something else. Once in Brooklyn, I got myself into a terrible spin. It was my own fault: I was walking. You don't walk in the USA. I was crossing roads, walking past buildings, looking at the passers-by. And, from one street to another, the buildings, roads and passers-by were all identical—at least, they seemed to be. I turned right and left, retraced my steps and pressed forward, but each time I found the same brick houses, the same white steps in front of the same doors, the same children playing the same games. At first, I enjoyed this; I had discovered the city of absolute equivalences. Universal and commonplace, I had no more reason to walk on *this* sidewalk than on *the same one* a hundred blocks away. The wave of stone, a thousand times recommenced, carried me onward, made me share in its inert renewal. What gradually wearied me was this constant advancing *to get nowhere*; I speeded up until I was almost running and yet I remained on the same spot. Suddenly, I was aware of a massive rejection: all these mass-produced blocks, all these sections of street, running along side by side, resembled each other further in being equally empty of me—except, that is, for one, which was in no way different from the others, and in which I had no more reason to be than in the neighbouring segments; and which, for unknown reasons —or for no reason at all—tolerated my presence. Suddenly, my movements, my life and even my weight seemed illegitimate: I wasn't a real person since I had no particular reason to be at this point of the forty-second parallel than any other. And yet I was a singular, irreducible individual, since my latitude and longitude defined me precisely. Neither everyone, nor someone, nor entirely some*thing*: a spatial determination, a guilty, contagious dream haunting the overheated asphalt in places, a lack of being, a flaw. A stubborn body in motion, my presence in the mechanical universe of repetition became a sheer accident, as mindless as my birth. Ubiquity would have saved me; I had to be legion, to stride along a hundred thousand sidewalks at once: that alone would have enabled me to be any old stroller in any old street in Brooklyn. Being unable either to leave myself behind or multiply, I hurled myself into the subway. I came back to Manhattan and, in my hotel, rediscovered my ordinary reasons for being—in no way compelling, but human.

There is no subway for the young Gorz, and no hotel or reason for being. Even in his room, he is outside; hence, he is illegitimate everywhere. And mystified to his bones: he believes he can escape his insignificant persona by parading the disgust it inspires in him; but it is, first and foremost, that disgust that lends him his singularity; the particularity of intellectuals is nothing other than their futile desire for universality.

But he has just finished his philosophical treatise. He steps back to look at it and the entire mystification disappears; universal thinking has narrowed and condensed; it has assumed a particular countenance: it looks like him. He is at the origin of a supernumerary object, this bunch of typewritten sheets, and, in the process, he has imprisoned himself in it. For a long time, the others have claimed to see the whole of him in his commonest gestures—his way of eating, of sitting, of opening a telegram. 'Oh, that really is you; that's you all over; I really see you in that; what you're doing there, that's pure Gorz.' God knows, it irritated him. But what has he just done, if not make a large-scale gesture of this kind that has now closed around him? The others will be only too happy. They will lean over the transparent walls of his prison and *recognize* him: 'that way of writing, old pal, that way of correcting yourself, of feeling your way into the subject, putting your toe in the water before you jump in, that is you, that really is you, it's you to a T; and these ideas, old chap, my dear old chap, that really is Gorz, it's pure Gorz and no mistake!' A devil in a bottle. He really has just one single approach to opening a tin can, other people's thoughts or an umbrella; a single approach to entering the mind of a seventeenth- century philosopher or the flat of a fellow student or a young woman. He re-examines the sentences in his book one by one: gestures, gestures, gestures! Gorz is there, before his very eyes, stretching out his long neck, pinching his thin lips: the Gorz that eternity will make of him.[8] All in all, he has tried to live and he has failed. He knows now that he was forced to fail and, moreover, that he was secretly resolved to do so.

At this precise moment, the Voice struck up. A little, barely intelligible murmur, born of anxiety and recrimination, ruminating on this surprising, yet foreseen defeat. The Voice acknowledges a simple fact: it's him, it definitely is him, it's his spitting image. This is enough to change everything: it was the others who claimed to know this parasite that was growing fat on his acts; the universal gaze of the Indifferent passed through him like light through a windowpane. He is suddenly there, opaque and unwieldy: 'Admit it! You've seen him, you've spoken to him, we know. Your line of defence won't convince anyone; we know when and where you met. The game's up.' The voice begins to confess: 'Yes, all right. I know him better than anyone. I've always known him. I'll tell you what I know about him.'

Wasn't I right a moment ago when I said one should speak of oneself in the plural? There are two people living off this poor unfortunate: there is Universal Man, that elusive, well-armed tyrant, and then there is the other one, the one left over. *One* makes oneself *a certain*

---

8 Sartre alludes here to the first line of Stéphane Mallarmé's 'Le tombeau d'Edgar Poe' ['The Tomb of Edgar Poe', in Sara Sigourney Rice (ed.), *Edgar Allan Poe: A Memorial Volume* (Baltimore: Turnbull Brothers, 1877)—Trans.]

Gorz by trying just to be Man; and, to be absolutely truthful about it, one tries to become *the whole of Man* because one refuses to be a certain Gorz. Yet who is refusing to be Gorz but Gorz himself? This refusal explains and defines him. If one *could accept* being—or, in other words, accept having been—the long-necked miser who wants to preserve his futile universality; if one spoke of him constantly; if one enumerated all his particular obstinacies; if, instead of passing through him, the intellectual gaze *saw into his soul,* wouldn't this 'eccentric' disappear, along with the stubborn negation that was the source of his eccentricity? It would not, admittedly, be future Man that came to take his place, but another individual whose basic obstinacies would merely risk being more positive. What would be gained? Is the game worth the candle? It is, in fact, too late to count the profits and losses: the voice is speaking, the undertaking has begun. The Traitor has chosen his own particularity as his goal.

It is not a question of knowing that particularity, nor entirely of changing it, but, *first and foremost,* of changing oneself by the will to know it. The Indifferent one does not have the foolish plan of depicting himself: he wants to modify the fundamental relationship that binds him to Gorz. When he turns towards the child, the adolescent that he was, when he interrogates his persona, his investigation is, in itself, an action: he suddenly halts his headlong flight, he forces himself to view himself without disgust; he brings his taste for totalizations to bear upon himself and, for want of being the whole of mankind, aspires first to become for himself *the whole of Gorz.*

This is not so simple: having neglected himself for so long, being in the midst of himself is like being a Robinson Crusoe on a desert island. How can he find the lost paths?—everything is covered in vines and briars. One can still latch on to memories, but what is a memory? What is the truth of this inert little picture? And what importance does it have? Is it the past exploding in the present like a bomb? Is it the present dressing itself up as the past? Or both? These two questions must have replies: *who* is this Gorz that I am? Who has made me in such a way that I both am Gorz and so fiercely refuse to be? But how are we to decide? Where are the tools for such a decision? Of course, there is no shortage of answers: there are tried and tested methods that offer themselves in haste and even perform little test demonstrations to show their efficacy: 'Your class,' says the one,

is completely decadent. Without principles or hope, it expends all its energies just keeping itself in being and no longer has the heart or, if you prefer, the naivety, to undertake anything new: your indifference is an expression of its anxious uncertainty. Existence seems purposeless to you because bourgeois life no longer has any meaning. Don't look anywhere else for the origins of your philosophical malaise: the bourgeoisie no

longer even has confidence in its ancient idealism, it attempts to hide it beneath old glad rags.
But you have held these worn-out fabrics in your
hand and seen how threadbare they are; you are
still disgusted with them, though you aren't able
either to be content with these outworn notions
or to find a new form of thinking.

He listens, he agrees, but he is not entirely convinced.
He has no difficulty conceding that he is a young bourgeois. Without needs, entirely abstract, 'a pure consumer
of water, air, bread and the labour of others, reduced to
an acute awareness of the contingency of all that sur-
rounds him.' But he knows lots of other bourgeois of his
age who are not like him. Admittedly, he could, without
abandoning the method, recover the historical and social
circumstances that may explain his peculiarities: he
informs us himself that he is Austrian, half-Jewish, that
he had to leave Austria at the time of the *Anschluss* and
that he lived for some years in Switzerland. He is persuaded that these factors have some influence on his cur-
rent attitude. But *what sort of influence*? And how is it
exerted? And, at a more general level, is there anything
more surprising or obscure than the action of people,
events or objects on the development of a human being?
All around him, everyone is in agreement: we are condi-
tioned. He cannot find anyone to doubt the existence of
this conditioning or to question its nature; these are
things that are handed down from father to son; the

arguments begin when they try to classify the various conditions and determine their importance. But all these people are inheritors: these presuppositions, these allegedly obvious facts are part of a very ancient heritage that each generation hands on to the next and that no one has ever catalogued exhaustively. The Indifferent one, by contrast, has inherited none of their convictions: the Exile from all groups must also be an exile from all ideologies. When he comes to consider both that he is 'the son of a Jew' and that he has an 'acute awareness of the contingency of everything', he wonders at the isolation, opacity and lofty irreducibility of these two facts that are so different: looking at them naively, you would say they were two miniature cities surrounded by ramparts and ditches; each is painted on an old canvas confined within a frame, both are hanging from the picture rail: between them *there is no visible path* because they do not exist in the same world. He is not, however, unaware that people come and go in their own little personal museum, that they move from a Circumcision to a Flagellation without even looking for the artists' names and say, '*This* is the cause of *That*, I am the unfortunate product of my race, of my father's Judaism, of the anti-Semitism of my schoolmates,' as though the true connection between these mysterious images of himself were quite simply the wall on which the paintings that enclose them are hung. But when he thinks of the peaceful self-assurance of these heirs, he falls into the profoundest bewilderment.

It is at this point that the other method offers itself, that strange dogmatism based on an absolute scepticism: does he remember his earliest years, the estrangement from the Jew she had married that his mother felt—and managed to inspire in him—the unbearable tension within the family group, the severe training he was made to undergo as soon as he could speak? Let him ask then whether he was not the victim of an abusive, castrating mother and whether he shouldn't date from that obscure time, from that distractedly experienced oppression, the appearance of the 'complexes' that cut him off from the world today. Isn't 'he', ultimately, the honorary Aryan, the persona an insulted wife wants to impose on her son because she reproaches a certain Israelite constantly with having been the only husband she could find? The docility of a moulded child might be said to survive in the adult in the form of apathy.

To which he replies that his upbringing did, in fact, leave him with complexes: his mother tried to turn him into the Other that he in part became; in his earliest years he suffered, as he does now, from a worried, zealous indifference. But he cannot manage to understand how these famous 'complexes' persist: he was apathetic at eight, and he is apathetic today. *Is it the same apathy?* Has it been preserved by an inert perseverance of being? But he will not believe so easily in human passivity: all his experience rejects this ever so convenient idea and the metaphysics that underpins it. Will he, rather, admit that he has nurtured and coddled his complexes; that he indulges them, fattens them up; that the adolescent and the adult have, by a kind of ongoing creation, taken over, re-emphasized and enriched the first characteristics of the child? In that case, he might be said to bear the responsibility for everything: it would be he, on a daily basis, who would be making himself indifferent.

He cannot reach a conclusion so quickly: none of these interpretations is entirely satisfactory, none is entirely clear in his eyes. A betrayer once again, like Hans Christian Andersen's child who sees that the emperor has no clothes, he draws up the inventory of our philosophical heritage, finds the coffers empty and ingenuously says so. Why, indeed, would he have himself interrogated by other people's methods, why would he give himself up to the psychiatric or Marxist police? It is, in fact, down to him to call these investigative procedures into question in the question he asks about himself. This Oedipus directs his investigation on to his own past and the validity of his memories, on to the rights of experience and the limits of reason—in a word, on to the legitimacy of the prophetic gifts claimed by our Tiresiases. But he turns his back on the universal: as regards method, he invents one by reflecting on his own case and the proof of that method will lie in its success. To bring himself to light as a particular totality, he has to confine himself within the experience of his particularity; he has to invent himself by inventing his own questioning and the means to respond to it. The Traitor wipes the slate clean and starts himself over again: this is what he gives us today: the opportunity to read a *radical* book.

For a long time we have listened to 'His Master's Voice'. Now it is Gorz speaking: the end of the monologue returns to its beginning, enwraps it and absorbs it. The meaning of the work appears now in full daylight. It was at first a question asked, in the shadows, by *no one*: on what conditions will the man known as Gorz be able to say 'I'? But immediately afterwards, an as-yet-indistinct being emerges from the darkness: it is not just a question of determining these conditions; the book becomes Gorz's living effort to fulfil them. *He* knows now that *he* will have done nothing if he does not wring the neck of the Vampires that wash him, clothe him and fatten him up, in order to grow fat on him: the first act that will be born on its own from my hands, that will depend on itself alone and on the obstacles to be surmounted, that will fold back on itself to lay hold of itself and control itself—it is this act that will say my first 'I'; this imperceptible sliding of an action against itself *will be me*. And what is preventing him from acting? He knows this too: it is the over-hasty desire to be prematurely universal. He repeatedly tells himself now that his future action will necessarily make use of *his* eyes, *his* mouth, *his* arms, that it will have the look of *his* face about it. And, above all, that he will be more strictly defined each day by the ephemeral agitation that his action conveys to the surrounding objects. Looked at from the outside, this is all a man is: an anxiety working over material within the limits of a strictly defined area. Old indi-vidual projects impose their individuality on a new project that goes back over all the others and indi-vidualizes them the more. *I* am this constant toing-and-froing. If he acts, he will be *himself*; but, if he is to act, he has first to *accept* himself. What is preventing him from doing so? What underlies his futile desire for universality? He discovers a heap of rubbish piled up in his heart: his childhood. He sets about breaking it down, but his efforts are not sufficient. He can no longer conceal from himself that he is perpetually reinventing his bastardy, the burden of his old miseries and infirmities. Because he cannot be everything, it is he *today* who pitches himself into a haughty passivity, to let everyone understand that he is externally determined and does not consent to this. It is he who annihilates himself of his own free will or, at least, who absents himself, leaving it to the habits that others have ingrained in him to keep him walking upright, performing the natural, social functions of his body. It is he who, in all freedom, has decided, like Saint John of the Cross, but without mysticism, that he will never do anything, so as freely to 'be nothing at all'. Is he, then, free? Of course he is: he has never doubted it. They have fabricated him, marked him and poured him into the plaster mould—*and* he is free? Yes: unfree or free will are one and the same thing where he is concerned. How can this be? He will try to say why, to explain why to *himself*, but his aim remains a practical one. The issue for him is to find the dialectical movement that is able to totalize the changing relations between past, present and future, between objective and subjective, between being and existence, between the apparatuses and freedom, so as to be able both to assert himself and to dissolve himself endlessly to the point where at last a genuine impulse is generated in his heart that is harrowing, that comes out through his hands and finds completion outside him in that holocaust of objects we call an *act*.

This is his task and he has just understood it. He puts down what he has understood on paper and, at that very moment, he notices that his innermost desire leaves his heart through his hands; that he is *already* embarked on an undertaking, that the words of today, yesterday and last month gather together and form themselves to reflect his new face to himself; that he is currently unmaking himself by words, in order one day to be able to make himself by acts; that this destruction is creating him, that it is determining him irreversibly; that it is transforming him gradually into that incomparable being of one sort or another that we each are for ourselves during the sleep of our Vampires; that he has at last 'taken the plunge', 'got himself involved' and condemned himself, whatever he may do, to have no other springboard again but himself. This is the moment: *hic Rhodus, hic salta*. His undertaking now takes on a different coloration; it takes on the thousand inner recesses of consciousness, the thousand circuits of reflection; it rubs against itself, feels itself, sees itself: the undertaking was the Voice. The Voice recognizes itself: in it, action discovers itself and says 'I'. *I* am creating this book, *I* am searching for myself, *I* am writing. Somewhere, a hollow-eyed chap sighs, intimidated: 'How pompous it is to talk in the first person!' And then he dissolves and Gorz appears: I am Gorz, *it was my voice* that was speaking, I write, I exist, I suffer myself and make myself—I have won the first round.

Is it worth shouting 'victory'? Who is Gorz, after all? A 'man of no social importance', a failed aspirant to universality who has left behind abstract speculation to become fascinated, instead, with his insignificant person. What has been gained by this? Where is the progress? I do not imagine that Gorz will reply to this question, but we can answer it for him. For we have followed this fantastical Cuvier[9] step by step as he found a bone, reassembled the animal from that minute vestigial element and ended up noticing that the reconstructed beast was actually himself. The method was valid for him alone—this he has said and re-said a hundred times; he was able to test it out only on his own case. But we have followed him; we have understood the meaning of his acts at the same time as he did. We have watched his experiments and seen the muscles being reborn around the knucklebone; we have seen the organism being gradually reconstructed and

---

9 Baron Georges Cuvier (1769–1832): perhaps the foremost comparative anatomist of his day. [Trans.]

seen the author and the book being produced by each other. Now, what we understand belongs to us; the Gorz approach is ours; when he attempts to interpret his life by the Marxist dialectic and by psycho-analysis, without every *entirely* managing to do so, his failure is our concern; we shall know how to attempt the experiment and we know the outcome in advance. And when he asks his own object—namely, himself—to devise his method for him, we immediately grasp the significance of this peculiar endeavour: for we are his fellows inasmuch as each of us is, like him, a unique anybody. What then is this object that turns itself into a subject under the appellation 'method'? Is it Gorz, or you and I? You are not 'Indifferent ones'; you will have other questions to ask yourselves about yourselves. In inventing *himself,* Gorz has not absolved you of the duty of inventing *yourselves.* But he has proved to you that totalizing invention was possible and necessary. Closing the book, every reader is consigned back to their own brush land, to the poisonous trees that people their own jungle. It is for them to cut their own ways through, to clear a path, to chase off the Vampires, to break out of the old iron stays, the old, worn-out actions to which resignation, fear and self-doubt have confined them. Can we be said to have rediscovered the universal by concentrating on the particular? No, that would be too much to hope for. We are no longer entirely animals, though we are not quite human beings. We have not yet turned to our advantage that appalling catastrophe that has befallen certain representatives of the animal kingdom: namely, thought. In short, we shall remain, for a long time yet, stricken mammals. This is the age of fury, fetishes and sudden terrors; universality is merely a dream of death amid separation and fear. But our world has been changing in the last few decades; reciprocity is being discovered even in the depths of hatred; even those who like to exaggerate their differences are clearly trying to conceal a basic identity from themselves. This agitation that is so novel, this modest, but strenuous attempt to communicate across the incommunicable is not the insipid—and always rather foolish—desire for an inert and already achieved universality. It is what I would call, rather, the movement of universalization. Nothing is possible yet; no agreement is in sight between the laboratory animals. We are separated by our universals, which afford constant opportunities for individual massacres. But if one of us turns away, anxiety-ridden, from the Idea and rejects abstract thinking; if one of us re-examines his singularity *in order to overcome it*; if one of us tries to recognize his loneliness in order to escape it, somehow to build bridges—in a strange, trial-and-error language similar to the one the aphasic reinvents—between the islets of our archipelagos; if one of us replaces our intransigent loves—that are really masked hatreds—with firm preferences; if one of us searches in the always singular, time-specific circumstances to unite with others, of whom he barely approves and who disapprove of him, to make the realm of Injustice a little less unjust, he will force the others to reinvent this same assiduous effort, to unite by recognizing their diversity. This is what Gorz has attempted: this traitor has smashed the tablets of the Universal, but he has done so to recover the movement of life, that slow universalization that is achieved by the affirmation and transcendence of the particular. The immediate consequence is that, at the very moment when he can at last say, *I* am doing this, *I* am responsible for it, he realizes that he is addressing *us*. For there are only two ways of speaking about oneself today: the third-person singular and the first-person plural. You have to be able to say 'we' if you are to be able to say 'I': this much is beyond dispute. But the converse is also true: if some tyranny, in order first to establish the 'we', deprived individuals of subjective thought, then the whole of inwardness would disappear at a stroke and, with it, relationships of mutuality: *they* would have won a definitive victory and we would never stop trotting round the experimental maze, crazed rodents in the grip of Vampires.

Gorz's book concerns us all. If at first he stammers and doesn't know where he's going, if he is perpetually transforming himself and if we feel his icy fever in our hands, if he contaminates us without seeing us and if, last of all, he addresses himself directly and intimately to every reader, this is because he is altogether shot through with the movement that drives us today, the movement of our age. Radical and modest, vague and rigorous, commonplace and inimitable, this is the first book *from after the defeat*. The Vampires created a memorable mayhem;

they crushed hope. We have to get our breath back, play dead for a while and then raise ourselves, leave the killing fields and begin everything again; we have to invent new hope, to try to live. The great massacres of the century have made a corpse out of Gorz: he has revived by writing an Invitation to Life.

Foreword to André Gorz, *Le Traître*
(Paris: Edition de Seuil, 1958)

✳

THE CONSPIRACY BY PAUL NIZAN

Nizan speaks of youth. But a Marxist has too much of a sense of history to describe an age of life in general, such as Youth or Maturity, the way these parade before us in Strasbourg Cathedral when the clock strikes noon.[1] His young people are assigned historical dates and ascribed to class backgrounds. They, like Nizan himself, were twenty years old in 1929, in the 'boom years' of that post-war period that has just ended. They are bourgeois; the sons, mostly, of that upper middle class that entertains 'anxious doubts about its future', of those 'rich tradespeople who brought up their children admirably', but who had ended up respecting only the things of the mind,

> without thinking that this ludicrous veneration
> for the most disinterested activities of life ruined

---

1 The Cathedral's famous astronomical clock incorporates figures representing the different ages of life which, at various different times of day, pass before the figure of Death. [Trans.]

everything, and that it was merely the mark of their commercial decadence and of a bourgeois bad conscience of which as yet they had no suspicion.[2]

Wayward sons, who had been diverted 'out of the paths of commerce' towards the careers of 'creators of alibis'. But there is in Marx a phenomenology of economic essences: I have in mind particularly his admirable analyses of commodity fetishism. In this sense, we can find a phenomenology in Nizan. In other words, he identifies and describes, on the basis of social and historical data, that essence-in-motion that is youth—a faked, fetishized age. It is in this complex proportioning of history and analysis that the great value of his book lies.

Nizan lived his youth to the full. When he was immersed in it, when it limited his horizons on every side, he wrote, in *Aden, Arabie*, 'I was twenty. I won't let anyone tell me it's the best time of life.'[3] It seemed to him then that youth was a *natural* age, like childhood, though much unhappier; and that responsibility for his woes had to be laid at the door of capitalist society. Today, he looks back over it and judges it with brutal frankness. It is an artificial age, an age that has been constructed and that one constructs, an age whose very structure and existence depend on society. It is the age

2 Paul Nizan, *The Conspiracy* (London: Verso, 1988), p. 68.

3 Paul Nizan, *Aden, Arabie* (New York: Columbia University Press, 1986), p. 59 (translation modified).

of inauthenticity *par excellence*. The twenty-year-old workers, who 'already have mistresses or wives, children, a profession . . . in short a life',[4] are protected from it by their misfortunes, their cares and their struggles to make a living—these young workers who, when their adolescence comes to an end, become young men, without ever having been 'young people'. But Lafforgue[5] and Rosenthal, students and scions of the bourgeoisie, live this great period of bloodless *ennui* to the full. Their grim frivolity and aggressive futility derive from the fact that they have no calls upon them and are by nature irresponsible. They 'are improvising' and nothing can claim their commitment, not even their membership of extremist parties: 'these diversions . . . had no great consequences for the sons of bankers and industrialists who could always return to the embrace of their class.'[6] They are wise, perhaps, if these improvisations were merely the product of a rapid contact with reality. Their actions lead nowhere and they forget them immediately. Their initiatives are entirely insubstantial; they know this and it is what gives them the courage to take action, even though they feign ignorance on that score. What else could their ventures be called, serious and frivolous as they are, but 'conspiracies'? But Lafforgue and Rosenthal are not *Camelots du roi*:[7] young bourgeois can come and

---

4 Nizan, *The Conspiracy*, p. 71.

5 Sartre misspells the name of the character Laforgue. [Trans.]

6 Nizan, T*he Conspiracy*, p. 228.

7 The Camelots du roi were a violent grouping of the extreme Right within the monarchist Action française movement. [Trans.]

make their conspiracies at the other end of the political spectrum, even in the parties of grown men. We can appreciate all that this fine word 'conspire' implies in the way of whisperings, little mysteries, hollow pretensions and fictitious perils—flimsy intrigues that are, in the end, mere play. And the great 'Dostoevskian' plot hatched by Rosenthal is mere play; all it will leave behind are two incomplete and entirely uninteresting files at the bottom of a drawer; and the manufactured love Rosenthal feels for his sister-in-law, itself an aborted conspiracy, is also fevered, angry play. And from play, it is a short leap to play-acting: they are lying to themselves because they know they are running no risk; they are trying in vain to frighten themselves; in vain—or almost— to deceive themselves. I think I can sense what great, mute sincerity of effort, physical suffering and hunger Nizan would set against their idle chatter. In fact, Bernard Rosenthal, who has, out of anger and idleness, gone through the irreparable motions of suicide, will know no other reality but his own death throes. They alone will show him—though too late—that he has 'missed love . . . that he no longer even loved Catherine and he was going to die cheated'. Yet these young people show the external signs of goodwill: they want to live, love, rebuild a crumbling world. But at the heart of this goodwill is that abstract, self-assured frivolity that cuts them off from the world and from themselves: 'their politics is still based only upon metaphors and shouts.'[8] This is because

---

8 Nizan, *The Conspiracy*, p. 48.

youth is the age of resentment. Not the age of the great anger of suffering humanity: these young people define themselves in relation to their families; they '[tend] to confuse capitalism with grown-ups'; they think they are moving towards a 'world destined for great metamorphoses',[9] but above all they want to give their parents some trouble. The young man is a product of the bourgeois family, his economic situation and worldview are exclusively family-centred.

These young people will not all make evil men. But Nizan shows that from this age, which Comte termed 'metaphysical', one exits only by revolution. Youth doesn't carry its solution within it: it has to crumble and wither; either the young man dies, like Rosenthal, or he is, like Pluvinage, condemned by his inferiority complex within the family to drag out an eternal, miserable adolescence. Nizan sees things going as badly awry in youth as they do for Freud in childhood; the pages in which he shows us Lafforgue's painful transition to adulthood are among the finest in the book.

I don't think Nizan wanted to write a novel. His young people are not novelistic: they don't do very much and aren't greatly differentiated from one another. At times they seem mere expressions, among so many others, of their families or their class. At other times, they are the tenuous thread linking events. But this is deliberate. In Nizan's eyes, they deserve no better; later he will make

---

9 Nizan, *The Conspiracy*, p. 49 (translation modified).

them human beings. Can a Communist write a novel? I am not convinced that he can: he doesn't have the right to become his characters' accomplice. But to find this a good and beautiful book, it is enough that we encounter on every page the haunting evocation of this unhappy, guilty age of life; it is enough for it to be a harsh, true testimony to the time when 'the Young' group together and feel good about themselves, when young men believe they have *rights* because they are young, the way taxpayers believe they have because they pay their taxes or fathers because they have children. It is a joy to rediscover, behind these derisory heroes, the bitter, gloomy personality of Nizan, the man who has not forgiven his youth: to rediscover, too, his beautiful, terse, carefree style; his long Cartesian sentences that collapse in the middle as though unable to support themselves, then take off again suddenly and finish up in the air; and those oratorical flights that suddenly stop short and give way to a curt, frosty judgement. Not a novelist's sly, concealed style, but a combative style, a weapon.

November 1938

✳

PAUL NIZAN

I

Feeling bored one day, Paul Valéry went over to the window and, gazing into the transparency of a pane, asked, 'How to hide a man?' Gide was present. Disconcerted by this studied laconicism, he said nothing. Yet there was no lack of possible answers: any method would do, from poverty and hunger to formal dinners, from the county jail to the Académie française. But these two excessively renowned bourgeois had high opinions of themselves. Each day they buffed up their twin souls in public and believed they were revealing themselves in their naked truth. When they died, long afterwards, the one morose, the other contented— both in ignorance—they had not even listened to the young voice crying out for all of us, their grand-nephews: 'Where has man hidden himself? We are stifling; we are mutilated from childhood: there are only monsters!'

The man denouncing our actual situation in these terms more than suffered in his own skin: while alive, there was not an hour that he did not run the risk of ruin. Dead, he faced an even greater danger: to make him pay for his clear-sightedness, a conspiracy of cripples tried to erase him from memory.

He had been in the Party for twelve years when, in September 1939, he announced he was leaving. This was the unpardonable crime, this sin of despair that the God of the Christians punishes with damnation. The Communists do not believe in hell: they believe in oblivion. It was decided that Comrade Nizan would be consigned to oblivion. One of many exploding bullets had hit him in the back of the neck, but that liquidation satisfied no one: it was not enough that he had ceased to live; he had to have never existed. They persuaded the witnesses to his life that they had not really known him: he was a traitor, a Judas; he worked secretly for the Ministry of the Interior and receipts had been found there bearing his signature. One comrade volunteered an exegesis of the works he had left behind, discovering in them an obsession with treason. 'How can an author who puts informers in his novels know about their ways,' asked this philosopher, 'unless he were an informer himself?' A profound argument, one must admit, but a dangerous one. The exegete has, in fact, himself become a traitor and has just been expelled; should we criticize him now for having projected his own obsessions on to his victim?

At any rate, the trick worked: the suspect books disappeared; the publishers were intimidated and left them rotting in cellars, as were the readers, who no longer dared ask for them. This grain of silence would germinate. Within ten years it would produce the most radical negation: the dead man would exit from history, his name would crumble into dust, his very birth would be excised from our shared past.

The odds were with them initially: a grave- robbery at night in a poorly guarded cemetery was no great task. If they lost the first phase of the battle, it was because they were too contemptuous of us. Blinded by mourning and glory, the Party intellectuals saw themselves as a chivalric order. They referred to each other as 'the permanent heroes of the age' and it was around this time, I think, that one of my former students informed me, with sweet irony, 'We Communist intellectuals suffer, do you see, from a superiority complex!' In a word, subhumans unaware of their subhumanity. Hence their arrogance carried them so far as to try out their slanders on Nizan's best friends: to test them, as it were. The encounter proved decisive: challenged publicly to produce their evidence, they scattered in disarray, blaming us for never trusting them and for really not being very nice.

The second round in this battle spelled defeat for us: to confound them was a small matter; we needed to convince, to push home our advantage, to cut off our enemies' retreat. Our victory frightened us: at bottom we quite liked these unjust soldiers of Justice. Someone said, 'Don't push it, they'll end up getting annoyed.' We heard no more of the story, but it did the rounds of the Communist Party by word of mouth and new recruits in Bergerac and Mazamet learned in dispassionate but absolutely certain terms of the ancient crimes of an unknown by the name of Nizan.

When I think of it, our negligence seems suspect; at a pinch, I will admit we had honestly assumed that his innocence as a man had been re-established. But his works? Was it acceptable for us to do nothing to rescue them from oblivion? It was their aim to be disagreeable: that is their greatest strength; and I am certain at present that we found them so. I recall, indeed, that we had acquired beautiful, new souls, so beautiful that I still blush to think of it. Not wanting to waste anything, the Nation decided to entrust to us those empty, insatiable pools in which it had no interest: pools of buried pain, the unsatisfied demands of the deceased—in short, all that is beyond recovery. These martyrs' merits were ascribed now to us; alive, we received posthumous decoration. We were, all in all, honorary dead men: a whispering campaign dubbed us Righteous; smiling, frivolous and funereal, we took this noble vacuity for plenitude and concealed our unparalleled promotion beneath the simplicity of our manners. Alongside whisky, Virtue was our chief diversion. We were every-one's friends! The enemy had invented classes in order to ruin us: in defeat, he took them with him. Workers, bourgeois and peasants all communed in the sacred love of the Fatherland. In the authorized circles, we thought we knew that self-sacrifice was rewarded in cash, that crime did not pay, that the worst does not necessarily happen and that moral advance brings technical progress. We proved by our very existence and self-conceit that the bad are always punished and the good always rewarded. Wreathed in glory and pacified, the Left had just entered upon the inexorable death throes that were to see it perish thirteen years later to the strains of military bands. Idiots that we were, we thought it was in fine fettle. Soldiers and politicians came home from Britain and Algeria; they crushed the Resistance before our eyes and spirited away the Revolution and we wrote in the newspapers and our books that everything was in fine order: our souls had absorbed the exquisite essence of these annihilated movements into themselves.

Nizan was a killjoy. His was a call to arms and hatred. Class against class. With a patient, mortal enemy, no quarter can be given: it is kill or be killed, there is no middle way. And no time for sleep. All his life, with his graceful insolence and his eyes lowered to his fingernails, he had repeated, 'Don't believe in Father Christmas.' But he was dead. The war had just ended. In every French hearth, shoes and boots were laid out and Father Christmas was filling them with tins of American food. I am sure that those who thumbed through *Aden, Arabie* or

Antoine Bloyé[1] at that time quickly broke off reading with lordly pity: 'pre-war literature, simplistic and decidedly passé'. What need had we of a Cassandra? Had he lived, we thought he would have shared in our new subtlety or, in other words, our compromises. What had preserved his violent purity? A stray bullet, no more and no less. That was nothing to boast about. This wicked corpse was gently chuckling to himself: in his books he had written that, past the age of forty, a French bourgeois is merely a carcase. And then he disappeared. At thirty-five. At present we, his classmates and comrades, bloated with that flatulence we call our souls, are running about the town with garlands for both Right and Left. And we are forty. Protecting innocence is our job; we are the just and we dispensed Justice. But we left *Aden, Arabie* in the hands of the Communists because we loathed all those who disputed our merits.

This attitude is an offence in French law: refusal to come to the assistance of a person in danger. If we had not morally liquidated this former colleague, it was because we did not have the means to do so. The rehabilitation was a farce. 'Talk, talk, that's all you can do.'[2]

---

1 Paul Nizan, *Aden, Arabie* (Paris: Francois Maspero, 1960 [1931]; *Aden, Arabie* (Joan Pinkham trans.) (New York: Monthly Review Press, 1960). Paul Nizan, *Antoine Bloyé* (Paris: Grasset: 1933); *Antoine Bloyé* (Edmund Stevens trans.) (Moscow: Co-operative Publishing Society of Foreign Workers in the USSR, 1935). [Trans.]

2 'Tu causes, tu causes, c'est tout ce que tu sais faire!' This is the refrain of the parrot in Raymond Queneau's *Zazie dans le métro* (Paris: Gallimard, 1959). [Trans.]

We talked: our beautiful souls spelled death for others; our virtue reflected our total impotence. It was, in fact, the job of the young to resurrect Nizan the writer. But the young people of the day—today quadragenarian carcases—gave no thought to that. Having just escaped an epidemic, what did the endemic disease of bourgeois death matter to them? Nizan asked them to look into themselves at a point when they believed they could at last look outwards. Of course they would die. 'Socrates is mortal.' 'Madame is dying, Madame is dead': they had been given some famous passages to learn at school: *Le Lac*, a sermon by Bossuet.[3] But there is a time for everything, and this was the time for living because for five years they had thought they were going to die. As adolescents they had been stunned by defeat: they had been heartbroken at no longer being able to respect anyone—either their fathers or the 'best army in the world' that had run away without fighting. The biggest-hearted had given themselves to the Party, which had repaid them royally: with a family, a monastic rule, tranquil chauvinism and respectability. In the aftermath of war, those young people went wild with pride and humility: they found pleasure in a sudden passion for obedience. I have said they were contemptuous of us all—by way of compensation. They twisted the arm of tomorrow to make

---

3 'Le lac', a poem by Alphonse de Lamartine (1790–1869), is one of the classics of French poetry routinely learned by French schoolchildren in this period. Similarly, the sermons of Jaques-Bénigne Bossuet (1627–1704) were taught as models of French prose style. [Trans.]

it yield a radiant socialist future; one can imagine how the brassy song of these birds drowned out the thin, chill voice of Nizan, the short-lived voice of death and eternity. Other adolescents found their relaxation in cellars: they danced, made love, went to each other's houses and threw their parents' furniture out of the windows in great, revolving potlatch ceremonies: in a word, they did all a young man can do. Some of them even read. In despair, of course. All of them were in despair: it was the fashion. And despairing of everything, except of course of the vigorous pleasure of despairing. Except of life. After five years, their futures were thawing: they had plans, the guileless hope of renewing literature through despair, of knowing the weariness of great global journeys, of the unbearable tedium of earning money or seducing women or, quite simply, of becoming a despairing pharmacist or dentist and remaining one for a long time, a very long time, without any other care than those of the human condition in its generality. How joyful they were! Nizan had nothing to say to them: he spoke little of the human condition and much of social matters and our alienations; he knew terror and anger better than he did the *douceurs* of despair; in the young bourgeois of his acquaintance he hated the reflection of himself, and, whether they were despairing or not, he despaired of them. His books were kept for the lean years, and rightly so.

Then, at length, came Marshall: the cold war hit this generation of dancers and vassals like a blow to the heart.

We old-timers took a bit of a battering, as did our virtues. 'Crime pays. Crime is rewarded.' With the return of these fine maxims, our beautiful souls perished in a dreadful stench. And good riddance to them. But our juniors paid for everyone. The night-clubbers became dumbfounded, old young men. Some are going grey, some balding, others have a paunch. Their relaxed attitude has frozen into inertia. They do what has to be done, and do it simply; they earn their corn, own a Peugeot 403 and a country cottage, have a wife and children. These young men were getting ready for life, they were 'starting out': their train came to a stop somewhere in the countryside. They will go nowhere now and do nothing. Sometimes a confused memory comes back to them from the glorious turbulent years; when this happens, they ask themselves, 'What did we want?' and cannot remember. They are well-adapted, yet suffer from a chronic maladaptation that will kill them: they are tramps without poverty; they are well fed, but they perform no service. I can see them at twenty—so lively, so joyous, so eager to relieve the old guard. I look at them today, their eyes ravaged by the cancer of astonishment, and I think to myself that they did not deserve this fate. As for the faithful vassals: some have not renewed their vows of fealty, others have fallen to a lower rank of vassalage. They are all wretched. The first group buzz around at ground level, never able to land: dismayed mosquitoes who have lost everything, including weight. The second group, sacrificing their organs of locomotion, have taken root in the sand: the slightest breath of wind can whip up these plants into a swarm. Nomadic or sedentary, they are united in stupor: where did their lives go? Nizan has an answer. For the desperate and for the vassals. Only I doubt whether they are willing or able to read it: for that lost, mystified generation, this vigorous dead writer tolls the knell.

But they have twenty-year-old sons, our grandsons, who register their defeats and ours. Until recently, the prodigal sons told their fathers where to get off, packed up and joined the Left. The rebel, following the classical pattern, became an activist. But what if the fathers are on the Left? What is to be done? A young man came to see me: he loved his parents, but, he said severely, 'They're reactionaries.' I have aged and words have aged with me: in my head, they are as old as I am. I mistook him. I thought I was dealing with the scion of a prosperous family that was rather sanctimonious, with free-market beliefs perhaps, voting for Pinay.[4] He put me right: 'My father's been a Communist since the Congress of Tours.' Another, the son of a socialist, condemned both the SFIO[5] and the CP: 'The one lot are traitors,

4 Antoine Pinay (1891–1994): a French conservative politician. He served as Prime Minister of France in 1952. [Trans.]

5 SFIO: Section Française de l'Internationale Ouvrière—the French Section of the Workers' International—was founded in 1905. A French socialist political party, it was designed as the local section of the Second International. After the 1917 October Revolution, it split (during the 1920 Tours Congress) into two groups, the majority creating the Section française de l'Internationale communiste (SFIC), which became the French Communist Party (PCF). [Trans.]

the others are in a rut.' And what if the fathers were con-
servatives? What if they supported Bidault?[6] Do we
believe this great upturned, worm-ridden cadaver, the
Left, can attract the young? It is a stinking, decaying carcase; the power of the military, and dictatorship and fas-
cism are being—or will be—born from its rotting
corpse; it takes a strong stomach not to turn away from
it. We, the grand-fathers, were made by the Left; we lived
by it; in it and by it we shall die. But we no longer have
anything to say to the young: fifty years of living in this
backward province that France has become is degrading.
We have shouted, protested, signed and signed again.
Depending on our habits of thought, we have declared,
'It is not acceptable . . .' or 'The proletariat won't stand
for . . .'. And yet, in the end, here we are; we have
accepted everything. How to convey our wisdom and
the fine fruits of our experience to these young
unknowns? From abdication to abdication we have
learned only one thing: our total powerlessness. Now, I
admit that this is the beginning of Reason, of the struggle for life. But we have old bones, and, at an age when
people are usually thinking about writing their wills, we
are discovering that we have achieved nothing. Shall we
tell them, 'Be Cubans, be Russians or Chinese, as you
like, be Africans'? They will tell us it is rather too late to

---

6 Georges-Augustin Bidault (1899–1983): a Christian-Democratic
French politician, active in the French Resistance during World War
II. After the war, he served as foreign minister and prime minister
on several occasions between 1945 and 1953. [Trans.]

change their place of birth. In short, accountants or tear-aways, technicians or teddy boys, they are battling alone and without hope against asphyxiation. And do not think those who choose job and family are showing resignation: they have turned their violence inwards and are destroying themselves. Reduced to impotence by their fathers, they cripple themselves out of spite. The others smash everything, hit anyone and everyone with everything and anything—a knife, a bicycle chain: to escape their malaise, they will send everything up in smoke. But nothing does go up in smoke and they end up at the police station, covered in blood. It was a great Sunday; next week they'll do better. Dishing out violence or taking it is all the same to them: there just has to be blood. In the daze that follows the brawls, only their bruises hurt; they have the funereal pleasure of empty minds.

Who will speak to these 'Angry Young Men'? Who can explain their violence? Nizan is their man. Year by year, his hibernation has made him younger. Not so long ago he was our contemporary; today he is theirs. When he lived we shared his anger, but, in the end, none of us performed 'the simplest Surrealist act' and now here we are, grown old. We have betrayed our youth so many times that mere decency demands we do not speak of it. Our old memories have lost their claws and their teeth. I must have been twenty once, but I'm fifty-five now and I would not dare write, 'I was twenty. I won't let anyone tell me it's the best time of life.' So much passion—and so lofty. Coming from my pen it would be demagogy. And then I would be lying: the unhappiness of the young is total, I know—I may perhaps have felt it once—but it is still human because it comes to them from human beings who are their fathers or their elders; ours comes from our arteries; we are strange objects half eaten away by Nature, by vegetation and covered with ants, we are like lukewarm drinks or the idiotic paintings that amused Rimbaud. Young and violent, the victim of a violent death, Nizan can step out of the ranks and speak to young people about youth: 'I won't let anyone . . .' They will recognize their own voices. To some he can say, 'Your modesty will be the death of you, dare to desire, be insatiable, let loose the terrible forces that are warring and whirling inside you, do not be ashamed to ask for the moon—we must have it.' To the others, 'Turn your rage on those who caused it, don't try to run away from your pain but seek out its causes and smash them.' He can say anything to them because he's a young monster, a fine young monster like them, who shares their terror of dying and their hatred of living in the world we have made for them. He was alone, became a Communist, ceased to be one and died alone near a window on a stairway. His life is explained by his intransigence: he became a revolutionary out of a sense of rebellion; when revolution was necessarily eclipsed by the war, he rediscovered his violent youth and ended as a rebel.

We both wanted to write. He finished his first book long before I penned a word of mine. At the point when

La Nausée[7] appeared, if we had valued such solemn presentations, *he* would have prefaced *my* book. Death has reversed the roles. Death and systematic defamation. He will find readers without my assistance: I have said who his natural readership will be. But I thought this foreword was necessary for two reasons: to show everyone the cunningly abject nature of his detractors and to warn the young to lend his words their full weight. They were once young and hard, those words; it is we who have caused them to age. If I want to restore to them the brilliance they had before the war, I must recall the 'marvellous age' of our refusals and make it live again, with Nizan, the man who said 'no' to the very end. His death was the end of a world: after him, the Revolution became constructive and the Left came to define itself by assent—to the point where, one day in Autumn 1958, it expired, with a last, dying 'yes' on its lips.[8] Let us attempt to recover the days of hatred, of unquenched desire, of destruction, those days when André Breton, barely older than we were, spoke of wishing to see the Cossacks watering their horses in the fountains of the Place de la Concorde.

---

7 Jean-Paul Sartre, La Nausée (Paris: Gallimard, 1938); Nausea (Lloyd Alexander trans.) (New York: New Directions, 1959).[Trans.]

8 26th September 1958 saw a 79.2 per cent referendum vote in favour of the Constitution of the new Fifth Republic with de Gaulle as president. [Trans.]

II

The error I want to avoid readers committing is one I made myself during his lifetime. Yet we were close—so close that we were sometimes mistaken for each other. In June 1939, Léon Brunschvicg[9] met the two of us at the publisher Gallimard's offices and congratulated me on having written *Les Chiens de garde*:[10] 'although,' as he told me without bitterness, 'you were rather hard on me.' I smiled at him in silence. Alongside, Nizan smiled too: the great idealist left without our having disabused him. This confusion had been going on for eighteen years; it had come to define us socially and, in the end, we accepted it. From 1920 to 1930, in particular, as schoolboys and then students, we were indistinguishable. Nevertheless, I did not see him as he was.

I could have drawn his portrait: medium height, dark hair. He squinted, as I did, but in the opposite direction, that is to say attractively. My divergent strabismus turned my face into an unploughed field; his was convergent, and lent him a mischievous faraway look, even when he was paying attention. He followed fashion closely, insolently. At seventeen, his trousers were so tight around the ankles that he had difficulty pulling them

9 Léon Brunschvicg (1869–1944): a French idealist philosopher who taught at the Sorbonne. Sartre and Nizan were both students of his and he supervised Simone de Beauvoir's thesis on Leibniz. [Trans.]

10 Paul Nizan, *Les Chiens de garde* (Rieder, Paris, 1932); *Watchdogs: Philosophers and the Established Order* (Paul Fittingoff trans.) (New York: Monthly Review Press, 1972). [Trans.]

on. A little later they flared into bell-bottoms, to the point where they hid his shoes. Then, all of a sudden, they turned into plus fours, up around his knees and billowing out like skirts. He carried a rattan cane and wore a monocle, wing collars or little round ones. He exchanged his iron-rimmed spectacles for enormous tortoise-shell ones which, with a touch of the Anglo-Saxon snobbery that raged among the youth of the time, he called his 'goggles'.

I tried to emulate him, but my family mounted effective resistance, even going so far as to bribe the tailor. And then someone must have put a spell on me: when I wore them, fine clothes changed into rags and tatters. I resigned myself to gazing at Nizan in amazement and admiration. At the École normale, no one gave much thought to how they dressed, with the exception of a few provincials who proudly wore spats and sported silk handkerchiefs in their waistcoat pockets. However, I don't remember anyone disapproving of Nizan's outfits: we were proud to have a dandy among us.

Women liked him, but he kept them at arm's length. To one who came right up to our very room and offered herself to him, he replied, 'Madam, we would be defiling each other.' In fact, he liked only girls, and he chose the virgins and the fools among them, drawn by the dizzying secret of stupidity—our only true profundity—and by the glossy brilliance of a flesh with no memories. Indeed, during the only liaison I ever knew him to have, he was constantly tormented by the most needless jealousy: he could not bear the thought that his mistress had a past. I found his behaviour quite incomprehensible, and yet it was very clear. I stubbornly insisted on seeing it as a personality trait. I also saw his charming cynicism and his 'black humour' as personality traits, together with his quiet, implacable aggressiveness; he never raised the tone of his voice; I never saw him frown nor heard him strain his voice: he would bend back his fingers and, as I have said, fall to contemplating his nails, loosing his violent remarks with a sly, deceptive serenity.

Together we fell into every trap there is: at sixteen, he offered me the role of superman and I eagerly accepted. There would, he said, be the two of us. Since he was a Breton, he gave us Gaelic names. We covered all the blackboards with the strange words R'hâ and Bor'hou. He was R'hâ. One of our classmates wanted to share our new-found status. We devised ordeals to test him. He had, for example, to declare out loud that the French army and the flag could go to hell; these remarks were not so daring as we imagined: they were commonplace at the time and reflected the internationalism and anti-militarism of the old pre-war days. However, the aspirant declined the task and the two supermen remained alone, eventually forgetting their superhumanity.

We would spend hours, days, strolling around Paris: we discovered its flora, its fauna and its stones, and were moved to tears when the first electric signs appeared; we thought the world was new because we were new in the world. Paris was the bond between us; we loved each other through the crowds of this grey city, beneath its light spring skies. We walked and talked; we invented our own language, an intellectual slang of the kind all students make up.

One night, the supermen climbed the hill of Sacré-Coeur and turning, saw a disorderly collection of jewels spread out beneath their feet. Nizan stuck his cigarette into the left-hand corner of his mouth, which he twisted into a horrible grimace, and announced, 'Hey, hey, Rastignac.' I repeated, 'Hey, Hey!' as I was meant to, and we walked down again, satisfied at having so discreetly marked the extent of our literary knowledge and the measure of our ambition. No one has written about those walks or that Paris better than my friend. Re-read *La Conspiration*[11] and you will recapture the fresh, yet quaint charm of that world-capital, quite unaware as yet that it would later become a provincial backwater. The ambition, the sudden mood-swings, the gentle, livid rages—I took it all in my stride. That was the way Nizan was, calm and perfidious, charming. That was how I loved him.

He described himself, in *Antoine Bloyé,* as 'a taciturn adolescent, already plunged into the adventures of youth,

---

11 Paul Nizan, *La Conspiration* (Paris: Gallimard, 1973); *The Conspiracy* (Quintin Hoare trans.) (London: Verso, 1989). [Trans.]

deserting childhood with a kind of avid exhilaration'.[12] And that is how I saw him. I experienced his taciturnity to my own cost. In *hypokhâgne*,[13] we fell out for six months, which I found painful. At the École normale, where we roomed together, he went for days without speaking to me. In the second year, his mood grew even darker: he was going through a crisis and could see no way out. He disappeared, and was found three days later, drunk, with strangers. And when my fellow students asked me about his 'escapades', I could answer only that he was 'in a foul mood'. Yet he had told me of his fear of death, but, being mad enough to believe myself immortal, I criticized him for this and thought that he was wrong: death wasn't worth a thought. Nizan's horror of death was like his retrospective jealousy—eccentricities that a healthy morale should combat.

When he couldn't stand things any longer, he left: he became a tutor with an English family in Aden. This departure scandalized the rest of us, rooted in the École as we were, but, since Nizan intimidated us, we found a benign explanation: love of travel. When he came back the following year, he did so at night when no one was expecting him. I was alone in my room. I had been plunged into a state of pained indignation since the previous day by the loose morals of a young lady from the

---

12 Paul Nizan, *Antoine Bloyé* (Paris: Grasset, 1933), p. 299. All translations from this work are by me [Trans.].

13 The first-year class of the two-year preparatory course for the arts section of the École normale supérieure. [Trans.]

provinces. He entered without knocking. He was pale, a bit breathless and rather grim. He said, 'You don't look too cheerful.' 'Neither do you', I replied. Whereupon we went off to have a drink and set the world to rights, happy that the good feeling was restored between us.

But this was simply a misunderstanding: my anger was a mere soap bubble, his was real. He gagged on the horror of returning to his cage with his tail between his legs. He was looking for the sort of help no one could give him. His words of hate were pure gold, mine were false coin. He ran off the very next day. He lived with his fiancée, joined the Communist Party, married, had a daughter, nearly died of appendicitis; then, after passing the *agrégation*, taught philosophy at Bourg and stood for election to parliament. I saw him less. I was teaching at Le Havre and there was also the fact that he had a family. His wife had given him a second child—a son—but it was mostly the Party that came between us: I was a sympathizer, but not an initiate. I remained his friend from adolescence, a petty-bourgeois that he liked.

Why did I not understand him? There was no lack of signs: why would I not see them? It was out of jealousy, I think: I denied the feelings that I couldn't share. I sensed from the very first that he had incommunicable passions, a destiny that would separate us. I was afraid and I blinded myself to these things. At fifteen, this son of a pious woman had wanted to take holy orders: I found out only many years afterwards. But I can still remember my scandalized bewilderment when, walking round the schoolyard with me, he said, 'I had lunch with the pastor.' He saw my stupor and explained in a detached tone, 'I may convert to Protestantism.' 'You,' I said, indignantly, 'But you don't believe in God.' 'Well, no,' he replied, 'but I like their morality.'

Madame Nizan threatened to cut off his allowance and the plan was dropped, but the moment had been enough for me to glimpse, beyond this 'childish whim', the impatience of a sick man writhing around to escape his pain. I did not want him to have this inaccessible pain: we shared superficial melancholies and that was enough; otherwise, I tried to force my optimism on him. I kept telling him we were free: he did not reply, but his thin, sidelong smile was eloquent.

On other occasions, he proclaimed himself a materialist—we were barely seventeen—and I was the one smiling scornfully. Materialist, determinist: he felt the physical weight of his chains; I did not want to feel the weight of mine. I hated him engaging in politics because I felt no need to do so myself. He was a Communist, then a follower of Georges Valois,[14] then a Communist again. It was easy to mock him and I wasn't slow to do so; in fact, these enormous swings were evidence of his stubbornness: there was nothing more excusable than

---

14 Georges Valois (1878–1945): a once prominent member of the monarchist Action française; the leader of France's first substantial fascist movement, Le Faisceau. [Trans.]

that he should hesitate between two extremes at the age of eighteen.

What did not vary was his extremism: whatever happened, the existing order had to be destroyed. For my part, I was quite happy at the existence of that order and the opportunity to hurl my bombs—my words—in its direction. This real need to unite with other men to move away the stones that were weighing them down seemed to me a mere dandy's extravagance: he was a Communist in the same way that he was a monocle-wearer, out of a trivial desire to shock.

He was unhappy at the École normale and I criticized him for it: we were going to write, we would write fine books that would justify our existences. Since I wasn't complaining, why was he? In the middle of the second year, he suddenly declared that literature bored him and he was going to be a cameraman; a friend gave him a few lessons. I was annoyed with him. In explaining to me that too much reading and writing had turned him against words and he now wanted to act on things and transform them into silence with his hands, he was, as I saw it, merely compounding his offence: this defector from the word could not condemn writing without passing sentence on me. It never occurred to me that Nizan was seeking, as we said at the time, his salvation, and these 'written cries' do not save.

He did not become a cameraman and I was delighted. But only briefly: his departure for Aden annoyed me. For him it was a matter of life and death, as I guessed. To reassure myself, I chose to see it as a further eccentricity. I had to admit to myself that I did not mean much to him, but, I ask myself today, whose fault was that? Where would you find a more stubborn refusal to understand and, hence, to help? When he came back from one of his binges, his panic-stricken flights, drunk and with death at his heels, I would welcome him tight-lipped without a word, with the dignity of an old wife who has resigned herself to such outrages, so long as it is understood that she is keeping score. It is true he was hardly encouraging. He would go and sit down at his table, gloomy, his hair tousled, his eyes bloodshot; if I happened to speak to him, he would give me a distant, hate-filled look. No matter, I still reproach myself for the fact that I had only these four words in my head: 'What an awkward so-and-so!' and that I never tried, even out of curiosity, to find an explanation for these escapades. His marriage I got all wrong. I was friendly with his wife, but bachelorhood was a moral principle with me, a rule of life. It could not, I assumed, be otherwise for Nizan. I decided he had married Rirette because that was the only way he could have her. In all honesty, I didn't realize that a young man in the grip of a dreadful family can break free only by starting one of his own. I was born to be a bachelor all my days. I did not understand that the single life weighed down the bachelor living at my side, that he detested casual affairs—because they have a taste of death about them—just as he detested travel, and that, when

he said 'man is a sedentary animal' or 'give me my field
. . . my needs, my men,' he was simply demanding his
share of happiness: a home, a wife and children.

When he published *Aden, Arabie*, I thought it a
good book and I was delighted. But I saw it only as a
lightweight pamphlet, a whirl of frivolous words. Many
of his classmates made the same mistake: we were set in
our thinking. For most of us, for me, the École normale
was, from the very first day, the beginning of indepen-
dence. Many can say, as I do, that they had four years of
happiness there. But here was a wild man flying at our
throats: 'The École normale . . . a ridiculous and more
often odious thing, presided over by a patriotic, hypo-
critical, powerful little old man who respected the military.' In his eyes, we were 'adolescents worn out by years
of lycée, corrupted by a classical education, and by bourgeois morality and cooking.'[15] We chose to laugh about
it: 'He didn't moan about the place when he was here,
did he? He seemed to have quite a good time with the
worn-out adolescents.' And we would recall our harmless
pranks, in which he had gladly taken part. Forgetting his
escapades, his scorn, and the great breakdown that took
him off to distant Arabia, we saw his passion merely as
excessive rhetoric. Personally, I felt foolishly offended
because he tarnished my memories. Since Nizan had

---

15 Paul Nizan, *Aden, Arabie* (Joan Pinkham trans.) (New York:
Columbia University Press, 1987), p. 61 (translation modified).
[Trans.]

shared my life at the École, he had to have been happy there, or else our friendship was dead even then. I preferred to rescue the past. I said to myself, 'It's all a bit over the top!' Today, I think our friendship was already dead, through no fault of our own, and that Nizan, consumed with loneliness, needed to be fighting among men rather than bandying words with an unfaithful and all-too-familiar reflection of himself. I was the one who maintained our friendship and embalmed it, by premeditated ignorance, by lying. In truth, our paths had always been moving apart. It has taken many years, and I have had to come at last to understand my own path through life, before being able to speak sure- footedly about his.

The more dismal life is, the more absurd is death. I do not claim that a man busy with his work and full of hope, cannot be struck, as if by lightning, by an awareness of death. I do say that a young man is afraid of death when he is unhappy with his fate. Before he is led by the hand to the seat that is kept for him, a student is the infinite, the undefined: he passes easily from one doctrine to another, detained by none of them; he finds all systems of thought equivalent. In fact, what we call 'classics' in school curricula is merely the teaching of the great errors of the past. Shaped by our republics in the image of Valéry's Monsieur Teste—that ideal citizen who never says or does anything but who knows what the score is all the same[16]—these young men will take twenty years

---

16 See Paul Valéry, *Monsieur Teste* (Jackson Matthews trans.) (New York: Alfred A. Knopf, 1947); also available in Jackson Matthews

to understand that ideas are stones, that there is an inflexible order to them and they have to be used for building. So long as worn-out old men, discreet to the point of transparency, carry bourgeois objectivity so far as to ask their students to adopt the standpoint of Nero, Loyola and Monsieur Thiers, each of these apprentices will take himself for pure Mind, that colourless, tasteless gas that at times expands to the galaxies and at others condenses into formulae. The young elite are everything and nothing: in other words, they are supported by the state and by their families; beneath this vaporous indistinctness their life burns away; suddenly pure Mind is brought up short against the stumbling block of Death. In vain does it try to encompass it in order to dissolve it: death cannot be thought. A body is struck down by an accident; a brute fact must put an end to the brilliant indeterminacy of ideas. This shocking realization awakens more than one terrified adolescent at night: against capital punishment and its incomprehensible particularity, universal Culture provides no defence. Later, when the individuality of his body is reflected in the individuality of the work he has undertaken, a young man will integrate his death into his life and view it as just one more risk among others—among all those that threaten his work and family. For those men who have the rare good fortune to be able to enjoy what they do, the final disaster, the less terrifying as one approaches

(ed.), *Collected Works of Paul Valery, Volume 6: Monsieur Teste* (Princeton, NJ: Princeton University Press, 1989). [Trans.]

it, is converted into the small change of everyday concerns.

I have described our common fate. That is nothing; but when the anxiety outlasts adolescence, when it becomes the profound secret of the adult and the mainspring of his decisions, the invalid knows his afflictions: his terror at the idea that he will soon be no more simply reflects his horror at still having to live. Death is the irremediable sentence; it condemns the wretched, for eternity, to have been only that: disgusting cala-mities. Nizan dreaded that fate: this monster crawled randomly among monsters; he feared one day he would burst and nothing would remain. He had known for a long time when he put these words into the mouth of one of his characters, that death was the definitive illumination of life: 'If I think about my death, it's for a good reason. It's because my life is hollow and death is all it deserves.' In the same book, Bloyé takes fright at 'the uniform countenance of his life . . . and [this fear] comes from a deeper region than the bleeding places in the body where the warnings of disease are formed.'[17]

What, when all is said and done, did he suffer from? Why did I sound ridiculous to him, more than to anyone else, when I talked about our freedom? If he believed, from the age of sixteen, in the inflexible chain

---

17 Nizan, *Antoine Bloyé*, p. 310. It would seem that Sartre misquotes Nizan here, who does not write, as Sartre suggests, of the 'visage uniforme de sa vie', but of the 'visage informe de toute sa vie'—the *formless* countenance of his whole life. [Trans.]

of causes, it was because he felt constrained and manip-
ulated: 'We have within us divisions, alienations, wars,
debates . . .' 'Every man is split between the men he can
be . . .'[18] Having been a solitary child, he was too conscious of his singularity to throw himself, as I did, into
universal ideas: having been a slave, he came to philosophy to free himself, and Spinoza provided him with a
model: in the first two types of knowledge, man remains
a slave because he is incomplete; knowledge of the third
type breaks down the partitions, the negative determi-
nants: so far as the mode is concerned, it is one and the
same thing to return to infinite substance or to achieve
the affirmative totality of one's particular essence. Nizan
wanted to beat down all walls: he would unify his life by
proclaiming his desires and assuaging them.

The easiest desire to name comes from sex and its
frustrated appetites: in a society that reserves its women
for old men and the rich, this is the first source of unhappiness for a poor young man and a premonition of his
future troubles. Nizan spoke bitterly of the old men who
slept with our women and sought to castrate us. But, all
in all, we were living in the age of the Great Desire: the
Surrealists wanted to awaken that infinite concupiscence
whose object is simply Everything. Nizan was looking
for remedies and took what he could find; through their
works he came to know Freud, who became part of his
pantheon. As revised by Breton and by a young writer

18 Nizan, *Aden, Arabie*, p. 65. [Trans.]

in peril, Freud looked like Spinoza: he tore away the veils and cobwebs, he imposed harmony on the enemies massacring each other in our tunnels, dissolved our raging monsters in light, and reduced us to the unity of powerful appetites. My friend tried him for a while, not without some felicity. Even in *Antoine Bloyé* we find traces of this influence. It gave us the following fine sentence, for example: 'As long as men are not entire and free, they will dream at night.' Antoine dreams: about the women he has not had and has not even dared to long for. On waking, he refuses to hear 'this voice of wisdom'. The fact is that 'the wakeful man and the sleeper seldom see eye to eye.'[19] Antoine is an old man, but here Nizan speaks from experience, I know; he used to dream, he dreamed until the day of his death: his wartime letters are filled with his dreams.

But it was only a working hypothesis, a temporary way of unifying himself. He adored the passing women in the street, those pale forms eclipsed by the light, by the smoke of Paris, those fleeting tokens of love; but he loved, above all, their being inaccessible to him: this well-behaved, literary young man intoxicated himself with privations; that is useful to a writer. But let us not suppose that he found chastity difficult to bear: one or two affairs—short and painful—and, the rest of the time, nice young girls whom he touched lightly as they slipped by. He would have been only too happy to find in him-

---

19 Nizan, *Antoine Bloyé*, pp. 260–1. [Trans.]

self merely a conflict between the flesh and the law; he would have decided the matter by finding the law guilty: 'Morality is an arsehole,' he used to say at twenty. In fact, taboos are more insidious, and our very bodies collude with them. Morality never showed itself but, with all women other than virgins, his unease was accompanied by a strong sense of revulsion. Later, when he had his 'field' and his 'men', he praised the beauty of the *whole* female body to me with a shocked, but precise, sense of wonder. I had wondered what had kept him from such a general discovery at the time of his devastating affairs. Now I know: it was disgust, an infantile repugnance for bodies he regarded as stale from past caresses. As adolescents, when we looked at women, I wanted them all; he wanted only one, and one who would be his. He could not conceive that it was possible to love unless one loved from dawn till night-time, or that there could be possession when you did not possess the woman and she did not possess you. He thought that man was a sedentary being and that casual affairs were like travel—abstractions. A thousand and three women are a thousand and three times the same, and he wanted one woman who would be a thousand and three times another; as a promise against death, he would love in her even the secret signs of fecundity.

In other words, the non-satisfaction of the senses was an effect, not a cause. Once married, it disappeared: the Great Desire fell back into line, became one need among others again, a need one satisfies poorly, too quickly or not at all. In fact, Nizan suffered from his present contradictions only because he deciphered them by the light of the future. If he formed the intention, one day, of killing himself, it was to put an immediate end to what he believed merely to be a recommencement. He was marked from childhood by Breton piety; too much or too little for his happiness; contradiction had settled beneath his roof. He was the child of old parents: the two adversaries had begotten him during a ceasefire; by the time he was born, they had resumed their quarrel. His father, first a manual worker, then an engineer on the railways, provided him with an example of adult, atheistic, technical thinking and, when he talked, betrayed a sorrowful loyalty to the class he had left behind. This mute conflict between a childish old *bourgeoise* and a renegade worker was something Nizan internalized from his earliest childhood; he made it the future foundation of his personality. However humble his position may be, the child of a charwoman has a part in the future of his family: his father makes plans. The Nizans had no future: the yardmaster was almost at the height of his career—what had he to look forward to? A promotion that was due to him, a few honours, retirement and death. Madame Nizan lived both in the crucial moment—when the onions have to be 'browned' or the juices 'sealed' in the chops—and in that fixed moment termed Eternity. The child was not far from his starting point and the family not far from its point of fall: carried along in this fall, he wanted to learn and build, whereas everything was visibly coming apart, even the marital quarrel. Externally, it had transformed itself into indifference; it existed nowhere, except within him. In the silence, the child heard their dialogue: the ceremonious, futile babble of Faith was occasionally interrupted by a harsh voice, naming plants, stones and tools. These two voices consumed each other. At first the pious language seemed to be winning out: there was talk of Charity, Paradise, of Divine Purpose, and all this eschatology did battle with the precise activity of the technicians. What was the point of building locomotives? There are no trains to heaven. The engineer would leave the house as soon as he could. Between the ages of five and ten, his son would follow him into the fields, take his hand and run along at his side. At twenty-five, he had fond memories of those men-only walks that were so obviously directed against the wife, against his mother. I note, however, that he gave his preference not to the Sciences but to the weary urbanity of the Word. A worker becomes an engineer, feels the deficiencies in his education and his son tries to get into the École Polytechnique; the pattern is a classic one. But Nizan showed a suspect repugnance for mathematics: he did Greek and Latin. As the stepson of a Polytechnique graduate, I had the same dislike, but for different reasons: we liked vague, ritualistic words, myths. Yet his father took his revenge: under the influence of his positivism, my friend sought to wrest himself from the baubles of religion. I have mentioned the stages of this release: the mystical transport—the last gasp of Catholicism—that almost took him into holy orders, his flirtations with Calvin, and the metamorphosis of his pious Catharism into political Manichaeism, royalism, and, in the end, Marxism. For a long time the two of us continued to use a Christian vocabulary: though atheists, we had no doubt we had been brought into the world to find our salvation, and, with a little luck, the salvation of others. There was only one difference: I felt certain I was one of the elect, Nizan often wondered if he were not damned. From his mother and Catholicism he got his radical scorn for the things of this world, the fear of succumbing to worldly temptations, and the taste—which he never lost—for pursuing an absolute Purpose. He was persuaded that, hidden within him, beneath the tangle of daily concerns, was a beautiful totality, flawless and unsullied; he had to hoe and weed, to burn the brushwood, and the indivisible Eternity would manifest itself in all its purity. And so, at this period, he regarded his father's job as manic, pointless agitation: the order of supreme purposes was being sacrificed to that of mere technical resources; man was being lost to the machine. He soon stopped believing in the white pills of life called souls, but he retained the obscure feeling that his father had lost his.

These ancient superstitions do not prevent you from living, *provided that you have the Faith*. But technology, ruled out of court, took its revenge by wringing the neck of religion. Nizan's dissatisfactions stayed with him, but they were rootless now and disconnected. Worldly activities are farcical, but, if nothing exists but the earth and the human animals scraping a living from it, then the children of men must take over and begin scraping: for there is no other occupation, short of doctoring the old Christian words. When Nizan offered me the strange prospect of becoming a superman, it was not so much pride that drove him as an obscure need to escape our condition. Alas, it was merely a matter of changing names. From that time on, until he left for Aden, he carried a constant millstone around his neck and kept on forging symbols of escape.

But one would understand nothing of Nizan's *angst* if one did not recall what I said earlier: he deciphered this arduous, disenchanted present, broken as it was only by brief periods of exhilaration, in the sinister light of a future that was nothing other than his father's past. 'I was afraid. My departure was a product of fear.' Fear of what? He says it right here in this book: 'mutilations . . . awaited us. After all, we knew how our parents lived.'[20] He expanded upon this sentence in a very fine, long novel, *Antoine Bloyé*, where he recounts the life and death of his father. As for Nizan, though he barely appears in the book, he continually speaks of himself: first, he is the witness to this process of decay; and second, Monsieur Nizan confided in no one—all the thoughts and feelings attributed to him are torn from the author's own person

20 Nizan, *Aden, Arabie*, p. 65. [Trans.]

and projected into that old, disordered heart. This constant dual presence is a sign of what psychoanalysts term 'identification with the father'.

I have said that, in his early years, Nizan admired his father, that he envied that sterile but visible strength, those silences and those hands that had toiled. Monsieur Nizan used to talk about his former comrades: fascinated by these men who knew the truth about life and who seemed to love each other, the little boy saw his father as a worker and wanted to be like him in every way—he would have his father's earthly patience. It would take nothing less than the obscure inner density of things, of matter, to save the future monk from his mother, from Monsieur le Curé, and from his own idle chatter. 'Antoine,' he said admiringly, 'was a corporeal being. He did not have a mind so pure that it separated itself from the body that nourished it and for so many years had provided it with the admirable proof of existence.'[21]

But the admirable man stumbled; suddenly, the child saw him begin to come apart. Nizan had committed himself unreservedly to his father: 'I shall be like him.' He now had to watch the interminable decomposition of his own future: 'That will be me.' He saw matter come to grief; the maternal prattle triumphed—and with it the Spirit, that foam that remained after the shipwreck. What happened? Nizan tells the story in *Antoine Bloyé*: for reasons I do not understand—because, while

---

21 Nizan, *Antoine Bloyé*, p. 273. [Trans.]

staying quite close to the truth in his book, he undoubtedly changed the circumstances—the man who served
as the model for Antoine sought, as early as forty years
of age, to take stock of his life. Everything had begun
with that false victory, a 'crossing of the line', at a time
when the bourgeoisie was promising everyone a 'great
future of equal opportunity,' a time when every work-
ing-man's son carried in his schoolbag . . . 'a blank cer-
tificate of membership of the middle classes.' Since the
age of fifteen, his life had been like the express trains he
would later drive, trains 'carried along by a force that was
all certainty and breathlessness'. And then, in 1883, he
graduated from the École des Arts et Métiers, eighteenth
out of a class of seventy-seven. A little later, at twenty-
seven, he married Anne Guyader, his yardmaster's
daughter. From that point on, 'everything was settled,
established. There was no going back.' He sensed this at
the very moment the *curé* united them and then he for-
got his worries: years passed, the couple went from town
to town, constantly moving house without ever settling.
Time wore on, and life remained provisional; yet every
day was like all the others in its abstraction. Antoine
dreamed, without too much conviction, that 'something
would happen.' Nothing happened. He consoled himself: he would show what he was made of in the real battles. But while he waited for the great events, the little
ones ate into him and imperceptibly wore him down.
'True courage consists in overcoming small enemies.'
Yet he rose irresistibly. First, he experienced 'the most

insidious peace', he heard the bourgeois siren song: he was able to derive from the false duties assigned to him—towards the Company, towards Society, *even* towards his former comrades—what might be called a vital minimum of good conscience. But 'the years piled up'; desires, hopes and memories of youth drove down 'into that shadowy realm of condemned thoughts into which human forces sink'. The Company devoured its employees: for fifteen years there was no man less self-aware than Antoine Bloyé: he was driven by, 'the demands, the ideas and the judgments of work'; he barely even scanned the newspapers: 'the events they speak of take place on another planet and are of no concern to him.' He passionately devoured 'descriptions of machines' in technical journals. He lived, or rather his body imitated the attitudes of life. But the mainsprings of his life, the motives for his action were not in him. In fact, 'complex powers prevent him from having his feet firmly set on the earth.' Changing just a few words, changing nothing, one could apply to him what Nizan writes about a rich Englishman in Aden: 'Each of us is divided among the men he might be, and Mr. C. has allowed to triumph within him that man for whom life consists of making the price of . . . Abyssinian leather go up or down . . . Fighting abstract entities such as firms, unions, merchants' guilds—are you going to call that action?'[22] Of course, Bloyé does not have so much power,

---

22 Nizan, *Aden, Arabie*, pp. 102–03. [Trans.]

but what of that? Isn't everything about his job abstract: the plans, the specifications, the paperwork—isn't it all *pre-ordained* somewhere else, a long way away, by other people? The man himself is merely a subsidiary of the company: this 'full employment' of himself leaves him both unoccupied and available. He sleeps little, works unstintingly, carries sacks and beams on his back, is always the last to leave his office, but, as Nizan says, 'all his work conceals his essential lack of an occupation.' I know. I spent ten years of my life under the thumb of a *polytechnicien*. He worked himself to death—or rather, somewhere, no doubt in Paris, his work had decided it would kill him.

He was the most trifling of men: on Sundays he would withdraw into himself, find a desert within and lose himself in it; he held on, though, saved by his somnolence or by rages of wounded vanity. When they retired him, it was, fortunately, during wartime: he read the newspapers, cut out articles and glued them into a notebook. At least he was straight about it: his flesh was abstract. For young Bloyé, however, the scandal lay in an unbearable contradiction: Antoine had a real body that was tough, capable and had once been eager; and that body imitated life: driven by distant abstractions, scuppering his rich passions, he transformed himself into a creature of the mind:

Antoine was a man who had a profession and a temperament, that was all. That is all a man is, in the world in which Antoine Bloyé lived. There are nervous shopkeepers, full-blooded engineers, morose workers and irascible solicitors: people say these things and think they have worked on defining a man; they also say a black dog, a tabby cat. A doctor . . . had told him, 'You're the highly-strung, full-blooded type, you are.' There, that said everything. Everyone could handle him like a coin of known value. He circulated with the other coins.[23]

The boy worshipped his father: I do not know if he would have noticed this inner wretchedness on his own. Nizan's misfortune lay in the fact that his father was better than the next man: after ignoring many danger signs, Monsieur Nizan came—too late—to see what he was and was horrified at his life; in other words, he saw his death and hated it. For almost half a century he had lied to himself, he had tried to persuade himself he could still 'become someone new, someone different, who would be truly himself.' He realized suddenly that it was impossible to change. This impossibility was death in the midst of life: death draws the line and tots up the score; but, for Nizan's father, the line was already drawn, the score already counted. This schematic, half-generalized creature shared a bed with a woman who was no more a particular person than he was, but more a relay station for the pious thoughts manufactured in Rome, and one who

---

23 Nizan, *Antoine Bloyé*, pp. 140–1. [Trans.]

had no doubt, like himself, repressed simple, voracious needs. He proclaimed their double failure to his frightened son. He would get up in the night:

> He carried his clothes over his arm and dressed at the foot of the staircase . . . He would go out . . . 'I'm surplus to requirements,' he would tell himself, 'I'm not wanted, I'm useless, already I don't exist; if I threw myself into the water no one would notice, there would just be the announcement of my death. I'm a failure, I'm finished . . .' He would come back in . . . shivering; he would draw his hand over his face and feel how his beard had grown during the night. Near the house, his wife and son, awakened, would be looking for him, calling to him: he could hear their high-pitched cries from a way off, but did not reply; he left them to worry till the very last moment, as if to punish them. They were afraid he had killed himself . . . When he got near them, stifling his anger, he would say, 'Haven't I the right to do as I like?' and he would go back up to his room without any concern for them.[24]

These nocturnal escapades are no novelist's invention: Nizan talked to me about his father and I know all this is true. Meditating on death inclines you to suicide,

---

24 Nizan, *Antoine Bloyé*, pp. 281–4. [Trans.]

out of a feverishness, an impatience. I ask you to imagine the feelings of an adolescent whose mother wakes him at night with the words, 'Your father isn't in his bedroom; this time I'm sure he's going to kill himself.' Death enters him, hunkers down at the crossroads of all his possible routes in life; it is the end and the beginning: dead in advance, his father wants to join the lists ahead of time—this is the meaning and conclusion of a stolen life.

But this paternal life occupied Nizan like a foreign power; his father infected him with the death that was to be his end. When this disenchanted old man—the doctors called him 'neurasthenic'—fled the house goaded by fear, his son feared two deaths in one: the first, in its imminence, presaged the other and lent it its aspect of horror. The father bayed at death[25] and the child died of fright each night. In this return to nothingness of a life that was nothing, the child believed he saw his destiny; 'everything was settled, established. There was no going back'. He would be this superfluous young man, then this empty shell, then nothing. He had identified with the strong maturity of another man; and when that man displayed his wounds, my friend was alienated from that mortal wretchedness. The engineer's unseemly nocturnal wanderings increased when Nizan turned

---

25 The French expression here is *hurlait à la mort*, which reflects a folk belief that dogs have an intuitive sense of death. A particularly lugubrious style of barking is thought to derive from the dogs' perception that someone in the surrounding area is dead or dying. [Trans.]

fourteen; now, between fifteen and sixteen, the adolescent took out an insurance policy on eternal life: in one last effort, he asked the Church to grant him immortality. Too late: when the faith is lost, disgust with one's times is not enough to restore it. He lived out his alienation: he believed himself to be another, interpreted every moment in the light of another existence. Everywhere he came upon the traps that had been laid for his father. Kindly and deceitful people got round him with flattery or by granting him false victories: academic honours, little gifts, invitations. The engineer's son would enter the teaching profession. And afterwards? Teachers, like railway yardmasters, move around a lot, pass hurriedly from town to town, take wives from the provincial lower middle class and align themselves, out of self-interest or weakness, with their masters. Are they less divided than the technicians? And which is better: building locomotives to serve a few overlords and the bourgeois state, or imparting a foretaste of death to children by teaching them dead languages, a loaded history and a mendacious morality? Do academics show more indulgence 'for their great pain, for the adventures coiled in the crevices of their bodies'? All these petty-bourgeois are alike: they have an imbecilic dignity imposed on them, they unman themselves, they have no sense of the real purpose of their work and they wake up at fifty to watch themselves die.

From the age of sixteen, I thought we were united by the same desire to write; I was wrong. As a clumsy hunter, I was dazzled by words because I always missed them; the more precocious Nizan had a game-bag full of them. He found them everywhere—in dictionaries, in books, even at large on people's lips. I admired his vocabulary and the way he dropped into the conversation, with ease and at the first attempt, the terms he had just acquired—among others, 'bimetallism' and 'percolator'. But he was far from fully committed to literature: I was inside it; the discovery of an adjective delighted me. For his part, he wrote better and watched himself write, doing so with his father's cheerless eyes. The words died or turned into withered leaves: can you justify yourself with words? The smouldering fires of death made literature seem a mere party game, a variant on canasta. It is quite natural for a teacher to write; he is encouraged to do so. And the same traps will work with both the engineer and the writer: flattery and temptation. At forty, all these flunkeys are mere shells of themselves. Valéry was buried beneath honours; he met with princes, queens and powerful industrialists and dined at their tables. And he did so because he was working for them: the glorification of the word serves the interests of people in high places; you teach people to take the word for the thing, which is not so costly. Nizan understood this: he was afraid of wasting his life gathering together mere wisps of voices.

He set about *repeating* his father's dark follies: he recommenced that man's nocturnal excursions and escapades. He would be walking in the street and suddenly 'he felt he was going to die (and) was suddenly a man apart from all the passers-by . . . It was a thing he knew in a single act of cognition, a thing of which he had a particular, perfect knowledge.'[26] It wasn't an idea, but 'an absolutely naked anxiety . . . far beyond all individual forms.' At such moments he believed he possessed a fundamental, material insight; he believed he understood the undivided unity of his body through the unity of its radical negation. But I don't think it was anything of the sort: we do not even have that, do not even have such unmediated communication with our nothingness. In reality, a shock had revived his old, learned pain-response: in him his father's life was draining away, the eye of *other death* reopened, tainting his modest pleasures: the street became a hell.

In those moments he loathed us: 'the friends he met, the women he glimpsed were life's accomplices, drawing drafts on time.' He would not even have dreamed of asking our help: we lacked awareness, we would not even have understood him: 'Which of these madmen loved him so shrewdly as to protect him from death?'[27] He fled our rapacious faces, our eager mouths, our greedy nostrils, our eyes ever set on the future. Gone missing. A three-day suicide, ending in a hangover. He was *reproducing* his father's night-time crises; these grew more

26 Nizan, *Antoine Bloyé*, p. 271. [Trans.]
27 Nizan, *Antoine Bloyé*, p. 276. [Trans.]

acute and ended in drink—and yet more words: I think he exaggerated the tragic element, being unable to achieve the perfect, gloomy sincerity of the fifty-year-old. No matter: his anxiety did not lie; and if you want to know the deepest, most specific truth, I would say that it was *this* and this alone: the death throes of an old man gnawing at the life of a very young one. He had fire and passion about him, and then that implacable stare froze everything; to judge himself on a daily basis, Nizan had placed himself beyond the tomb. In fact, he was going round in circles: there was, of course, the rush to get to the end, and the panic fear that he would do so; there was the time that was wearing away, 'the years piling up', and those traps he just managed to avoid, that manhunt, the sense of which he didn't quite understand; but there was also, in spite of everything, his muscles, his blood: how could you stop a well-fed young bourgeois from trusting in the future? He did have times of sombre enthusiasm, but his own excitement frightened him, aroused mistrust: what if it were a trap, one of the lies you tell yourself to choke back your anxiety and pain? The only thing he liked in himself was his revolt: it proved he was still holding out, that he was not yet on the track that leads, irresistibly, to life's sidings. But when he thought about it, he was afraid that his resistance might weaken: they have thrown so many blankets on me that they've almost got me; they will start again. What if I were to get used, little by little, to the condition they are preparing for me?

Around 1925–26, this was what he feared madly: habituation. 'So many ties to break, secret timidities to conquer, little battles to fight . . . One is afraid of being . . . unbearably singular, of no longer being just like anyone . . . false courage waits for great opportunities; true courage consists in defeating the little enemies each day.'[28] Would he manage to defeat these gnawing enemies? And in five or six years' time, would he still be capable of breaking all these ties, which daily increased in number? He was living in enemy country, surrounded by the familiar signs of universal alienation: 'Just try, while still in your arrondissements and sub-prefectures, to forget your civic and filial obligations.'[29] Everywhere there were invitations to slumber, to abandonment, to resignation: he had got to the point of cataloguing his abdications: 'the terrible old habits'. He was also afraid of that alibi so dear to the cultured: the empty noise in his head of torn and precious words. Meditation on death has, in fact, other consequences, more serious than these intermittent conversations: it disenchants. I was running after sparks that for him were merely ashes. He wrote, 'I tell you, all men are bored.' Now, the worst damage done by boredom, 'that continuous forewarning of death', is to generate a by-product for sensitive souls: the inner life. Nizan feared his very real loathings might end up by giving him an over-refined subjectivity, and

---

28 Nizan, *Aden, Arabie*, p. 83. [Trans.]

29 Nizan, *Aden, Arabie*, p. 83. [Trans.]

he was afraid that he might lull his grievances to sleep with the purring of 'empty thoughts, and ideas that are not ideas at all'. These aborted offspring of our impotence deflect us from facing up to our wounds, our bleeding. But Nizan, with his eyes wide open, felt sleep rising in him.

So far as the sons of the bourgeoisie are concerned, I think this revolt can be termed exemplary, because it has neither hunger nor exploitation as its direct cause. Nizan sees all lives through the cold window-pane of death: in his eyes, they become balance-sheets; his fundamental alienation is the source of his insight: he can sniff out any kind of alienation. And how serious he is when he asks each of us, in the presence of our death, like a believer, 'What did you do with your youth?' What a deep, sincere desire to knit together the scattered strands in each of us, to contain our disorders in the synthetic unity of a form: 'Will man never be anything but a fragment of man—alienated, mutilated, a stranger to himself; how many parts of him left fallow . . . how many things aborted!'[30]

These cries of protest on the part of a 'sub-human' form the outline in negative of the man he wanted to be. He put his mystical flights to one side, his taste for adventure and his word-castles. The inaccessible image remains simple and familiar: man can be said to be a harmonious, free body. There is a bodily wisdom—

---

30 Nizan, *Antoine Bloyé*, p. 137. [Trans.]

constantly stifled, but constantly present since Adam; 'in the most obscure part of our being are hidden our most authentic needs.' It is not a question here of being madly in love or of undertakings that exceed our powers: man is sedentary; he loves the earth, because he can touch it; he enjoys producing his life. The Great Desire was just empty words: *desires* remain, modest but concrete, balancing each other out; Nizan felt an affection for Epicurus, on whom he later wrote very well:[31] *there* was a man who spoke to everyone, to prostitutes and to slaves, and he never lied to them.

We may be reminded here of Rousseau and not without reason: out of loyalty to his childhood, Nizan the town-dweller retained a kind of rustic naturalism. We may also wonder how this noble savage could have adapted to the needs of socialist production and interplanetary nomadism. It is true: we shall not recover our lost liberty unless we invent it; there can be no looking back, even to gauge the extent of our 'authentic' needs.

But let us leave Epicureanism and Rousseau to one side: to do otherwise would be to take fleeting hints to extremes. Nizan began with individualism, like all the petty-bourgeois of his day: he wanted to be *himself* and the entire world was separating him from himself; against the abstractions and symbolic entities they tried to slip into his heart, into his muscles, he defended his

---

31 See Paul Nizan, *Les matérialistes de l'antiquité. Démocrite, Épicure, Lucrèce* (Paris: Maspero, 1965 [1938]). [Trans.]

own, individual life. He never wasted effort describing the fullness of moments or passions: for him it did not exist. It is what is stolen from us. But he said that love was true and we were prevented from loving; that life could be true, that it could bring forth a true death, but that we were made to die even before we were born. In this upside-down world, where ultimate defeat is the truth of a life, he showed that we often have 'encounters with death' and each time confused signs awaken 'our most authentic needs'. A little girl is born to Antoine and Anne Bloyé; she is doomed and they know it; grief draws closer together these abstract characters, who have been living in solitude despite being crowded together. For only a short while, the singularity of an accident will never be able to save individuals.

From the age of fifteen, Nizan had understood the key things about himself: this had to do with the nature of his suffering. Some alienations are, in fact, the more formidable for the fact that they are covered up by an abstract sense of our freedom. But he never felt free: there had been *possession*; his father's 'bungling unhappiness' occupied him like a foreign power; it imposed itself upon him, destroying his pleasures and impulses, governing by *diktat*. And one could not even say this wretched fate had been produced by the ex-worker; it came from all quarters, from the whole of France, from Paris. Nizan had tried for a time—in the days of mysticism, of R'hâ and Bor'hou—to struggle alone, by way of words and moral uplift, against his revulsions and the discords within him. But to no avail: the fabric of our social being crushes us. Spinoza came to his aid: you have to act on the causes. But what if the causes are not in our hands? He deciphered his experience: 'What man can overcome his dividedness? He will not overcome it on his own for its causes are not within him.' This is the juncture at which to bid a scornful farewell to spiritual exercises: 'I was under the impression that human life disclosed itself through revelation: what mysticism!'[32] It is clearly the case that one has to fight and that one can do nothing on one's own. Since everything comes from elsewhere—even the innermost contradictions that have produced the most singular features of one's character— the battle will be waged elsewhere and everywhere. Others will fight for him *there*; *here*, Nizan will fight for others: for the moment, it is simply a question of seeing clearly, of recognizing one's brothers-in-darkness.

As early as his second year at the École normale, he had been drawn to the Communists: in short, his decision was made. But decisions are taken in the night and we battle for a long time against our own will, without recognizing what that will is. He had to knock on all the doors, to try everything, to test out solutions he had long since rejected. He wanted, I think, to experience the good things of this world before making his vow of poverty. He left in order to bury his bachelor life. And

---

32 Nizan, *Aden, Arabie*, p. 85 (translation modified). [Trans.]

then the fear mounted and he had to break it off. Aden was his last temptation, his last attempt to find an individual way out. His last escapade too: Arabia attracted him in the same way as, on certain evenings, the Seine had attracted his father. Did he not later write of Antoine Bloyé that he 'would have liked to abandon this existence . . . to become someone new, someone foreign, who would really be himself'? He imagined himself '. . . lost, like a man who has left no address and who is doing things and breathing.' He had to get away from us and from himself.

We lost him, but he did not shake himself off. He was gnawed at now by a new abstraction: to run from one place to another, to chase after women was to hold on to nothing. Aden is a compressed version of Europe, heated to a white-hot temperature. Nizan one day did what his father—when still living—never dared: he took a car and set out on the road without a helmet at noon. They found him in a ditch, unconscious but unharmed. This suicide attempt swept away some old terrors. Coming round, he looked about him and saw 'the most naked state, the economic state'. The colonies lay bare a regime that is seen only through a mist in the home countries. He came back: he had understood the causes of our servitude; the terror within him became a force of aggression: it turned to hatred. He was no longer fighting insidious, anonymous infiltrations; he had seen exploitation and oppression in the raw and understood that his adversaries had names and faces: they were human beings. Unhappy, alienated human beings, no doubt, like his father and himself. But 'defending and preserving their unhappiness and its causes with cunning, violence, obstinacy and cleverness'. On the night of his return, when he came knocking at my door, he knew he had tried everything, that he was up against it, that all the exits were blind alleys except one: war. He came back to his enemies' heartland to fight: 'One must no longer be afraid to hate. One must no longer be ashamed to be a fanatic. I owe them some pain. They almost did for me.'[33]

It was over: he found his community and was received into it; it protected him from them. But, since I am presenting him here to the young readers of today, I must reply to the question they will unfailingly ask: did he at last find what he was looking for? What could the Party offer to this sensitive soul, wracked to the core of his being by the horror of death? We have to ask this conscientiously: I am telling the story of an exemplary existence, which is the absolute opposite of an edifying life. Nizan turned over a new leaf and yet the old man— the old, young man—remained. Between 1929 and 1939, I saw less of him, but I can give an impression of these meetings which, though shorter, are the more vivid for it. I am told people choose family ahead of politics today. Nizan had chosen both—together. Aeneas had

---

33 Nizan, *Aden, Arabie*, p. 159 (translation modified). [Trans.]

tired of carrying gloomy old Anchises for so long: with a heave of his shoulders he dropped him flat on his back; he became a husband and father in great haste, in order to kill his father. But fatherhood alone is an insufficient remedy for childhood. Far from it. The authority of the new head of the family condemns him to repeat the age-old childishnesses that Adam bequeathed to us through our parents. My friend knew the score: he wanted to strike a definitive blow against the father who, in the passage from father to son, is repeatedly murdered and repeatedly revived. To do so, he would become *a different person* and, through a public discipline, would take care to avoid family quirks. Let us see whether he succeeded.

The doctrine fully satisfied him. He detested reconciliation, and among conciliators he most detested Leibniz, their Grand Master. Forced by the syllabus to study the *Discourse on Metaphysics*, he took his revenge by making a talented drawing of Leibniz in full flight, wearing a Tyrolean hat, with the imprint of Spinoza's boot on his right buttock. From the *Ethics* to *Capital*, by contrast, the transition was easy. Marxism became second nature for Nizan, or, rather, became equivalent to Reason itself. His eyes were Marxist, and his ears too. And his head. He was at last able to explain to himself his incomprehensible wretchedness, the holes in his life, his anxiety: he saw the world and saw himself in it. But, above all, the doctrine—while lending legitimacy to his hatreds—

reconciled in him the opposing voices of his parents. Technical rigour, scientific exactitude and the patience of reason—everything was preserved. At the same time, the pettiness of positivism was overcome and its absurd refusal to 'know through causes'; the sad world of means—and of means to means—was left to the engineers. For the troubled young man trying to save his soul, there were absolute goals on offer: playing midwife to history, making revolution, readying Man to come into his kingdom. There was no talk of salvation or personal immortality, but survival, in fame or anonymity, was granted as part of a shared undertaking that ended only when the human race came to an end. He put everything into Marxism: physics and metaphysics, the passion for action and for rehabilitating his actions, his cynicism and his eschatological dreams. Man was his future: but this was a time for cleaving things apart; others would have the job of stitching them back together; to him fell the pleasure of merrily smashing everything to pieces for the good of humanity.

Everything suddenly took on substance, even words: he had distrusted them because they served bad masters. Once he could turn them against the enemy, everything changed. He used their ambiguity to confound, their dubious charms to beguile. With the Party's guarantee, literature could even become idle chatter; the writer, like the ancient sage, would, if he wanted, turn a triple somersault. All the words belonged to man's enemies; the Revolution gave permission to steal them; that was all.

But it was enough: Nizan had been pilfering for ten years and suddenly he came forth with the sum total of his thefts: his vocabulary. He understood his role as a Communist writer and understood that discrediting the enemies of man or discrediting their language were, for him, one and the same thing. It was 'no holds barred', the law of the jungle. The masters' Word is a lie: we shall take apart their sophisms and shall also invent sophisms against them; we shall lie to them. We shall even go so far as to clown around, so as to prove, as we speak, that the masters' speech is clownish.

These games have become suspect today: Eastern Europe is building; it has given our provinces a new respect for the 'trinkets of high-sounding inanity'.[34] I have said we were serious, caught between two kinds of false coin, one coming from the East, the other from the West. In 1930, there was only one sort and, with us in France, the Revolution was simply at the destructive stage: it was the intellectual's mission to spread confusion and muddle the threads of bourgeois ideology; marauding troops were setting fire to the brush and whole linguistic sectors were being reduced to ashes. Nizan seldom played the fool and had little time for sleight of hand. He lied, like everyone in that golden age, when he was quite certain he would not be believed: slander had just been born, a nimble, joyous thing verging on poetry.

---

34 The quotation is from Mallarmé, 'Plusieurs sonnets, IV', Œuvres complètes, p. 68. [Trans.]

But he found these practices reassuring: we know that he wanted to write against death, and death beneath his pen had turned words into dead leaves; he had been afraid of being duped, afraid of wasting his life toying with trifles. Now he was being told he had not been wrong, that literature was a weapon in the hands of our masters, but he was being given a new mission: in a negative period, a book can be an act if the revolutionary writer applies himself to de-conditioning language. Everything was permitted—even to create a style for himself: for the wicked, this would be a gilding of a bitter pill; for the good, it would be a call to vigilance: when the sea sings, do not jump in. Nizan studied the negative form: his hatred produced pearls; he took the pearls and cast them before us, delighted that it fell to him to serve common ends by producing so personal a body of work. Without changing its immediate target, his battle against the particular dangers menacing a young bourgeois became a sacred charge: he spoke of impotent rage and hatred; he wrote of the Revolution.

The writer, then, was made by the Party. But the man? Had he at last found 'his field'? His fulfilment? Was he happy? I do not believe so. The same reasons deprive us of good fortune as make us forever incapable of enjoying it. And then, the doctrine was clear and chimed with his personal experience: his alienations, being linked to the present structures of society, would disappear when the bourgeois class disappeared. Now, he did not believe that he would see socialism in his lifetime nor, even if he saw it in the last days of his life, that such a metamorphosis of the world would leave time to transform the old habits of a dying man. Yet he had changed: his old bouts of desolation never returned; he was never again afraid he was wasting his life. He had an invigorating violence about him, and felt joy: he accepted in good heart being only the *negative man*, the writer of de-moralization and de-mystification.

Was there enough in this to satisfy the serious child he had continued to be? In a sense, yes. Before he joined the Party, he clung to his rejections. He clung to the idea that, since he could not achieve true being, he would be empty: he would derive his sole value from his dissatisfaction, from his frustrated desires. But, sensing a torpor coming over him, he was terrified of letting go and of one day subsiding into consent. As a Communist, he consolidated his resistances: up until then he had continually feared that dunce, the 'social man'. The Party socialized him without tears: his collective being was none other than his individual person; it was enough merely that his restless agitations were now *sanctioned*. He saw himself as a monstrous, misbegotten thing; he was heaved on to the stage, where he showed off his wounds, saying, 'See what the bourgeois have done to their own children.' Once he had turned his violence against himself: now he made it into bombs which he hurled at the palaces of industry. The buildings sustained no damage, but Nizan found deliverance. He presided over a sacred fury, but he no more felt it than a fine singer hears his own voice; this *mauvais sujet* turned himself into a terrible object.

It was not so easy to free himself from death, or rather from the shadow it cast over his life. But the adolescent ravaged by an alien anxiety acquired, as an adult, the right to die his own death. Marxism revealed his father's secret to him: Antoine Bloyé's loneliness was the product of betrayal. This worker-turned-bourgeois thought constantly of:

> the companions he had had in the yards of the Loire and among the watchmen at the goods depots, who were on the side of the hirelings, on the side of life without hope. He said . . . something he would strive to forget, which would disappear only to reappear at the time of his decline, on the eve of his own death: 'So I am a traitor.' And he was.[35]

He had crossed the line, betrayed his class and ended up as a simple molecule in the molecular world of the petty-bourgeois. On a hundred occasions, he felt his friendlessness—one day in particular, during a strike, seeing the demonstrators marching by:

> These men of no importance bore far away from him the strength, friendship and hope from which he was excluded. That evening,

---

35 Nizan, *Antoine Bloyé*, pp. 135–6. [Trans.]

Antoine felt he was a man of solitude. A man without communion. The truth of life lay with those who had not 'succeeded'. They are not alone, he thought. They know where they are going.[36]

This renegade had fallen apart; now he was whirling around in the bourgeois pulverulence. He knew alienation, the misfortune of the rich, as a result of having thrown in his lot with those who exploited the poor. This communion of 'the men of no importance' could have armed him against death. With those men, he would have known the fullness of misfortune and friendship. Without them, he remained unprotected: dead before his time, a single blow of the scythe had severed his human bonds and cut short his life.

Was Mr Nizan really this tearful deserter? I do not know. At any rate, his son saw him that way: Nizan discovered or thought he discovered the reason for the thousand tiny resistances he put up against his father: he loved the man in him, but loathed the betrayal. I beg those well-intentioned Marxists who have studied my friend's case, and have explained it by the obsession with betrayal, to re-read his writings with open eyes, if they can, and not reject the glaring truth. This son of a traitor does, admittedly, often speak of betrayal; in *Aden* he writes, 'I could have been a traitor, I might have suffocated.' And in *Les Chiens de garde*, he writes: 'If we betray

---

36 Nizan, *Antoine Bloyé*, p. 207. [Trans.]

the bourgeoisie for humanity, let us not be ashamed to admit that we are traitors.' A traitor to men, Antoine Bloyé; a traitor still, in *La Conspiration*, the sad Pluvinage, the son of a cop and a cop himself. And what does it mean, then, this word repeated so often? That Nizan was in the pay of Daladier? When they speak of others, the right-thinking characters of the French Left are shamefully hungry for scandal; I know of nothing dirtier or more puerile, except perhaps 'decent' women gossiping about a free woman. Nizan wanted to write, he wanted to live: what need had he of thirty pieces of silver from secret political funds? But as the son of a worker who had become a bourgeois, he wondered what he might become: bourgeois or worker? His chief concern was undoubtedly this civil war within him; as a traitor to the proletariat, Mr Nizan had made his son a betraying bourgeois; this bourgeois-despite-himself would cross the line in the opposite direction: but that is not so easy. When the Communist intellectuals want a bit of fun, they call themselves proletarians: 'We do manual work in our garrets.' Lacemakers, so to speak. Nizan, more clear-sighted and more demanding, saw them—saw himself, indeed—as petty-bourgeois who had chosen the cause of the people. That does not actually close the gap between a Marxist novelist and an unskilled worker: they can exchange smiles from either side of the intervening gulf, but if the author takes a single step, he falls in. All this is true when we are speaking about a bourgeois who is the son and grandson of a bourgeois: against the fact of birth, fine feelings are powerless. But Nizan? He was close to his new allies by ties of blood: he remembered his grandfather who 'remained on the side of the hirelings, on the side of life without hope'; he had grown up, like the sons of the railwaymen, in landscapes of iron and smoke; yet a diploma in the 'liberal arts' had been enough to make his a lonely childhood, to force an irreversible metamorphosis on the whole family. He never crossed the line again: he betrayed the bourgeoisie without rejoining the enemy army and had to remain something of a 'Pilgrim' with one foot on either side of the frontier; right to the end he was the friend—but he never managed to become the brother—of 'those who have not succeeded'. It was nobody's fault but those bourgeois who had taken his father into their class. This discreet absence, this emptiness always troubled him a little: he had heard the bourgeois siren song. Retaining his scruples, he remained anxious: for want of participating in the 'communion of hirelings, of those who live without hope,' he never saw himself as sufficiently protected from temptations, from death; he knew the comradeship of fellow militants without escaping his loneliness, which was the legacy of a betrayal.

His life would not be stolen from him; released now from an alien death, he contemplated his own: it would not be the death of a railway yardmaster. But this negative man, robbed of the humblest plenitude, knew he would ultimately suffer an irreparable defeat. With his passing, nothing might be said to have happened but the disappearance of a refusal. All in all, a highly Hegelian demise: it would be the negation of a negation. I doubt if Nizan drew the slightest consolation from this philosophical view. He made a long journey to the USSR. On his departure, he had told me of his hopes: over there perhaps, these men were immortal. The abolition of classes closed up all the divides. United by a long-term undertaking, the workers would change themselves by death into other workers, and those into others in their turn; the generations would succeed each other, always different and always the same.

He came back. His friendship for me did not entirely exclude the propagandist's zeal: he told me the reality had exceeded all his expectations. Except on one point: the Revolution freed men of the fear of living, but it did not remove the fear of dying. He had questioned the best among them: they had all replied that they thought about death and that their zeal for the shared task gave no protection from that obscure personal disaster. Disabused, Nizan forever renounced the old Spinozist dream: he would never know that affirmative plenitude of the finite mode which, at the same time, shatters its own limits and returns to infinite substance. In the midst of the collective commitment, he would retain the particularity of his disquiet. He tried not to think of himself any more, and he succeeded, concentrating only on objective necessities: yet he remained, as a result of this hollow, indissoluble nothingness—this bubble of emptiness within him—the most fragile and the most 'irreplaceable' of human beings. Individualized in spite of himself, a few scattered phrases show that he ended up choosing the most individual solution: 'It takes a great deal of strength and creation to escape nothingness . . . Antoine understood, at last, that he could only have been saved by creations he had produced, by exercising his power.'[37] Nizan was not an engineer. Nor a politician. He wrote; he could exercise power only through the practice of style. He put his trust in his books: he would live on through them. Into the heart of this disciplined existence, which grew more militant each day, death injected its cancer of anarchy. This lasted somehow for ten years. He devoted himself to his party, lived a dissatisfied life and wrote with passion. From Moscow there came a squall—the Trials—which shook, but did not uproot him. He held out. But to no avail: this was an unblinkered revolutionary. His virtue and his weakness were that he wanted everything *right now*, the way young people do. This man of negation did not know renunciation of assent. About the trials he remained silent and that was all there was to it.

I regarded him as the perfect Communist, which was convenient: in my eyes, he became the spokesman for the Political Bureau. I saw his moods, illusions, frivolities and passions as attitudes agreed by the Party leadership. In July 1939, where I met him by chance for the last time, he was cheerful: he was about to take a

---

37 Nizan, *Antoine Bloyé*, p. 285. [Trans.]

ferry to Corsica. I read in his eyes the cheeriness of the Party; he spoke about war, expressing the view that we were going to escape it. I immediately translated in my head: 'the Political Bureau is very optimistic, its spokesman declares that the negotiations with the USSR will bear fruit. By the Autumn,' he says, 'the Nazis will be on their knees.'

September taught me it was prudent to dissociate my friend's opinions from Stalin's decisions. I was surprised by this. And annoyed: though apolitical and reluctant to commit myself in any way, my heart was on the Left, as was everyone's. Nizan's rapid career had flattered me; it had given me some sort of revolutionary importance in my own eyes. Our friendship had been so precious and we were still so often confused for one another that it was I too who wrote the foreign politics leaders in *Ce Soir*— and I knew quite a bit about all that! Now, if Nizan knew nothing, what a come-down: we were back to being a pair of real clots. Sent back to the ranks. Unless he had deliberately deceived me. This conjecture amused me for a few days: what a fool I was to have believed him; but this way he retained his high-flying role, his perfect insight into what in those days we called 'the diplomatic chessboard'. Deep down, I preferred this solution.

A few days later in Alsace, I learned from the newspapers that the spokesman for the Political Bureau had just left the Party, making a great splash about the break. So I had been wrong about everything, from the very outset. I don't know why I wasn't completely stunned by this news: perhaps my frivolousness protected me; and then, at this same time, I discovered the monumental error of a whole generation—our generation—which had actually been sleepwalking. Through a fierce period of preparation for war, when we thought we were strolling on the calm lawns of Peace, we were actually being impelled towards massacres. At Brumath I experienced our immense anonymous awakening; I lost my distinctiveness once and for all and was drawn in.[38]

Today I recall this learning experience without displeasure and I tell myself that at the same time, Nizan was engaged in *unlearning*. How he must have suffered! It is not easy to leave a party: there is its law, which you have to wrench from yourself if you are to break it, its people, whose beloved, familiar faces will become filthy enemy 'mugs', that sombre crowd continuing on its stubborn march which you will watch disappear into the distance. My friend became an interpreter: he found himself alone in the north of France among British soldiers: alone among the British, as he had been at the worst time of his life in Arabia, fleeing beneath the sting of the gadfly, separated from everyone and saying 'no'.

---

38 Sartre was at Brumath, Alsace, in November 1939 when he began writing the second of his surviving wartime notebooks, which were published as *Les carnets de la drôle de guerre* (Paris: Gallimard, 1995, second edition); *War Diaries: Notebooks from a Phoney War 1939–40* (Quintin Hoare trans.) (London: Verso, 1984). [Trans.]

He gave political explanations, of course. His former friends accused him of moralism; he criticized them for not being Machiavellian. He approved, he said, of the lofty cynicism of the Soviet leaders: all means were permitted when it came to saving the socialist fatherland. But the French Communists had neither imitated this cavalier attitude, nor understood that they had to distance themselves in appearance from the USSR; they were going to lose their influence for failing to put on a timely act of indignation.

He was not the only one to give these reasons—how frivolous they seem today! In fact, this recourse to Machiavelli was merely a riposte to his critics: Nizan was attempting to prove his realism; he was a tactician condemning a tactic: nothing more—and, above all, he didn't want anyone to think that he was resigning for emotional reasons or because his nerves were shot! His letters prove, on the other hand, that he was distraught with anger. We know the circumstances and documents better today, we understand the reasons driving Russian policy: I tend to think his decision was a headstrong one and that he should not have broken with his friends, with his real life. Had he lived, I believe the Resistance would have brought him back into the fold, like so many others. But that is none of my business: I want to show that he was cut to the quick, wounded to the heart, that his unexpected turnabout revealed his nakedness to him again, sent him back to his desert, to himself.

He was writing for *Ce Soir* at the time; he was put in charge of foreign affairs, where a single theme prevailed—union with the USSR against Germany. He had argued this so many times that he had become convinced of it. When Molotov and Ribbentrop were putting the last touches to their pact, Nizan, in his harshest tones, was demanding a Franco-Soviet *rapprochement* with menaces. In the summer of 1939, he saw some of the leaders in Corsica: they talked with him in a friendly way, congratulated him on his articles and, when he had gone to bed, held long secret meetings. Did they know what was in store for us? There is some chance they did not: the September revelation struck a holidaying Party like a thunderbolt. In Paris we saw journalists assuming the most serious responsibilities blindly and with a sense of dismay. At any rate, Nizan never doubted for a moment that he had been lied to. It pained him, not in his vanity, nor even in his pride, but in his humility. He had never crossed the class boundary—he knew; suspect in his own eyes, he saw the silence of his party bosses as a sign of the people's distrust. Ten years of obedience had not allayed it: they would never forgive this dubious ally for his father's betrayal.

That father had worked for others, for gentlemen who robbed him of his strength and life; against this, Nizan had become a Communist. Now he learned that he was being used as a tool, with the real objectives hidden from him; he learned that lies had been put into his mouth and he had repeated them in good faith: from him too, unseen, remote individuals had stolen his strength, his life. He had put all his obstinacy into rejecting the gentle, corrosive words of the bourgeoisie and, all of a sudden, in the Party of the revolution, he was back with what he feared most: alienation from language. Communist words, so simple, virtually raw—what were they? Leaking gas. He had written that his father '[had performed] solitary acts that had been imposed on him by an external, inhuman power, . . . acts that had not been part of an authentic human existence, that had produced nothing enduring. They were merely recorded in bundles of dusty files . . .'[39] At present, his actions as a militant came back to him and they were virtually identical to those of the bourgeois engineer: 'nothing enduring'; articles scattered in dusty newspapers, hollow phrases imposed by an external power, the alienation of a man to the necessities of international politics, a frivolous life emptied of its substance, 'the vain image of that headless human being walking in the ashes of time, with hurried tread, directionless and disorientated'.[40]

He came back to his eternal concern: he became politically active to save his life and the Party stole his life from him; he was fighting death and death was coming to him from the Party itself. He was, I think, wrong: it was the Earth that gave birth to the slaughter and it

---

39 Nizan, *Antoine Bloyé*, pp. 307–08. [Trans.]

40 Nizan, *Antoine Bloyé*, p. 310. [Trans.]

broke out in all parts at once. But I am relating what he felt: Hitler had a free hand now, he was going to hurl himself against us; Nizan, dumbfounded, imagined that our army of workers and peasants would be exterminated with the consent of the USSR. To his wife he spoke of another fear: he would return too late and exhausted from an interminable war; he would survive only to ruminate on his regrets and his rancour, haunted by the false coin of memory. Against these rediscovered threats, only revolt remained—the old desperate, anarchic revolt. Since human beings were betrayed on all sides, he would preserve the little bit of humanity that remained by saying 'no' to everything.

I know the angry soldier of 1940, with his prejudices, principles, experience and intellectual resources was not much like the young adventurer who set out for Aden. He wanted to be rational, to see things clearly, weigh everything up and maintain his links with 'those who have not succeeded in life'. The bourgeoisie awaited him, affable and corrupting: they had to be thwarted. Having been betrayed, as he saw it, by the Party, he felt anew a pressing duty not to betray in his turn; he persisted in calling himself a Communist. He pondered patiently how he was to correct the deviations without falling into idealism? He kept notebooks and logs; he wrote a great deal. But did he really believe he could redirect the inflexible thrust of these millions of human beings on his own? A lone Communist is lost. The truth of his last months was hatred. He had written that he wanted 'to fight real men'. At that juncture, he had in mind the bourgeois, but the bourgeois has no face: the person you think you detest slips away, leaving behind Standard Oil or the Stock Exchange. Right up to his death, Nizan harboured particularized grudges: out of cowardice, such and such a friend hadn't supported him; another had encouraged him to break with the Party, then condemned him for it. His anger was fuelled by some undying memories; in his mind's eye he saw eyes, mouths, smiles, skin tones, a harsh or sanctimonious look and he hated these all-too-human faces. If ever he had an experience of fullness, it was in these violent moments when, selecting these hunting trophies, his rage turned to delight. When he was totally alone, 'directionless and disorientated', and reduced to the inflexibility of his refusals, death came and claimed him. *His* death, stupid and savage, in keeping with his constant fears and forebodings.

An English soldier took the trouble to bury his private notebooks and his last novel, *La Soirée à Somosierra*, which was almost finished. The earth devoured this testament: when his wife, following precise instructions, tried to recover his papers in 1945—the last lines he had written about the Party, the war or himself—there was nothing left of them. Around this time, the slander against him began to be taken seriously: the dead man was found guilty of high treason. What a funny old life:

a life alienated, then robbed, then hidden, and saved even in death because it said 'no'. Exemplary too, because it was a scandal, like all the lives that have been lived, like all the lives that are manufactured today for young people; but a conscious scandal and one that publicly declared itself such.

Here is his first book. We thought he had been obliterated; he is reviving today because a new audience demands it. I hope we shall soon have restored to us his two masterpieces: *Antoine Bloyé*, the finest, most lyrical of funeral orations, and *The Conspiracy*. But it is no bad thing to begin with this raw revolt: at the origin of everything, there is refusal. So now, let the older generation withdraw and let this adolescent speak to his brothers: 'I was twenty. I won't let anyone tell me it's the best time of life.'

March 1960.
Foreword to Paul Nizan, *Aden, Arabie*
(Paris: Éditions François Maspéro, 1960).

A NOTE ON SOURCES

'Of Rats and Men'

Originally published as 'Des rats et des hommes' in *Situations IV* (Paris: Gallimard, 1964), pp. 38–84.

First published in English translation in *Portraits* (London: Seagull Books, 2009), pp. 45–112.

'*The Conspiracy* by Paul Nizan'

Originally published as 'La Conspiration par Paul Nizan' in *Situations I* (Paris: Gallimard, 1947), pp. 25–8.

First published in English translation in *Critical Essays* (London: Seagull Books, 2010), pp. 32–9.

'Paul Nizan'

Originally published as 'Paul Nizan' in *Situations IV* (Paris: Gallimard, 1964), pp. 130–88.

First published in English translation in *Portraits* (London: Seagull Books, 2009), pp. 179–265.